www.pippal.org

These books are available at special quantity discounts for educational needs. Please write to info@pippal.org

Jaswant Singh Khalra – The Valiant

For ages 12+

Written by: Gurmeet Kaur
Editorial Direction: Rafaqat Ali
Punjabi Translation: Parvesh Sharma, Gurmeet Kaur, Nirvair Singh
Illustrated by: Amandeep Singh
Art Direction: Gurmeet Kaur and Navkiran Kaur Khalra
Graphic Design: Gurdeep Singh Dhaliwal
Edited by: Shelby Steinhauer and Gayle O'Shaughnessy

Printed in China by Crash Papers on certified reforested, chlorine free paper with soy-based ink

First Edition: September, 2020 (Available in Punjabi & English)

ISBN: 978-0-9887101-9-1

“Until the lion learns how to write,
every story will glorify the hunter.”

African Proverb

ਦੀਵਾ ਮੇਰਾ ਏਕੁ ਨਾਮੁ ਦੁਖੁ ਵਿਚਿ ਪਾਇਆ ਤੇਲੁ॥
ਉਨਿ ਚਾਨਣਿ ਓਹੁ ਸੋਖਿਆ ਚੂਕਾ ਜਮ ਸਿਉ ਮੇਲੁ॥੧॥

The One *Naam* is my lamp
my sufferings its oil
the oil burnt into light
dispelling the darkness of death.

Guru Baba Nanak, SGGS: 358

THE VALIANT

JASWANT SINGH KHALRA

The story of one man's mission to find the disappeared sons and daughters of Punjab, and how the love of life or the fear of death couldn't stop him.

GURMEET KAUR

CONTENTS

Prologue

A Lamp is Lit

"There is a fable that when the sun was setting for the very first time, light was diminishing. As darkness set its foot on the earth, chaos ensued. 'What will happen when the sun sets, when the darkness spreads, and when no one can see? What will happen to us,' people lamented.

It is said that far away, in some hut, one little lamp lifted its head. The lamp proclaimed, 'I challenge the darkness. If not everywhere, then at least around myself, I will not let it settle. Around myself, I will establish light.' It is said that seeing it, another lamp in a hut close by raised its head, and then another one. Slowly the earth was lit by little lamps everywhere, and the darkness vanished.

Today, when darkness is falling over truth with all its might, my Punjab is like that little lamp challenging the darkness, and I pray that it will keep lighting the way for justice forever."

Jaswant Singh Khalra - Vaisakhi, April 1995, in his recorded speech at Gurdwara Ontario Khalsa Darbar, Mississauga, Canada.

ਬਾਬਾਣੀਆ ਕਹਾਣੀਆ ਪੁਤ ਸਪੁਤ ਕਰੇਨਿ॥

Stories of the glorious ancestors
inspire goodness in a child.

Guru Amardas, SGGS: 951

A VILLAGE NAMED KHALRA

Not So Long Ago

Jaswant Singh was born on November 2, 1952 in Punjab, in a village named Khalra. It is situated only three kilometers east of the border between India and Pakistan, exactly halfway between the cities of Lahore in West Punjab (Pakistan) and Patti in East Punjab (India).

Jaswant, whose name meant "the glorious one", was lovingly called Juss in his childhood. Little could anyone imagine what glory Juss was destined to achieve. Jaswant was the sixth of nine children born to Mukhtiar Kaur and her husband, Kartar Singh. They lived in their ancestral home with his grandmother Gulab Kaur, along with Jaswant's five sisters and three brothers.

In many ways, Juss's family was much like others in the village; they had a small piece of land that they farmed, and kept a few cows and buffalos to provide milk for their large family. Working hard and living simply, each family member helped with the household and with tending the farm and the livestock. In some ways, however, this family was very different. They were well-read, and they made education a priority.

Juss had a huge appetite for reading and listening to stories. He helped his father with chores after school, and in return, his father, whom he called *Bapu-ji*, shared stories of the great women and men of Punjab, especially from the *Majha* area, a region in the center of Punjab that extends from the river Beas to the northern banks of the river Jhelum. Often, he told these stories on their way back from the fields. Sometimes, when little Juss exhausted

his father, Juss would snuggle with his grandmother, *Bibi-Ji*, or his mother, *Maañ-Ji*, and ask for more. He could never get enough of these stories, nor did the family ever run out of them.

Perhaps Juss and his siblings inherited their love of stories from *Bapu-ji*, who did his *Gyani*, a graduate degree, in the Punjabi language, and who had worked as a clerk and a teacher at the Khalra High School. Or perhaps the love of stories came from the tradition of Punjab, the land of heroes, where tales of valor and chivalry have been passed down for generations through oral tradition, and where there are always children in each family who carry this tradition of heroism forward. Juss would surely be the one in his family.

Juss grew up hearing of Mai Bhago of Jhabal,* the woman warrior who, in the early eighteenth century, challenged the men who had abandoned the warfront. She led them back to the battlefield to fight and die in dignity defending Guru Gobind Singh, the tenth Sikh Guru. Jhabal was located only twenty-five kilometers from Khalra.

The story of the life of Bhai Taru Singh of Puhla also inspired Juss. Bhai Taru Singh gave his life but not his faith when the late eighteenth century governor of Punjab, Zakariya Khan, ordered him scalped alive for refusing forced conversion to Islam. Puhla was located some ten kilometers from Khalra.

Juss was fascinated by Lahore, where Bhagat Singh, a revolutionary and a freedom fighter, was martyred at the age of twenty–three in 1931. It was also in Lahore that Dulla Bhatti, a great folk hero

---

Jhabal: Full name Jhabal Kalañ, also known as Chabal

of about the same age, was hanged for revolting against undue taxation on the poor by Emperor Akbar in 1589. Lahore, too, was no more than twenty-five kilometers from Khalra. As he got to know a new hero every day, Juss marveled at the brave people of Punjab. He felt proud to belong to a land that had given birth to so many heroes, and all so close to his village.

Jaswant wondered if he, too, would also be a hero someday.

Jaswant Singh (left) at age seven with his siblings, Khalra, 1960 - Family collection

The Border

Juss was born in a Punjab, partitioned merely five years earlier, when the pain and suffering of the division was still fresh in the soil and in the hearts of his older siblings, parents, and grandparents.

Juss noticed that when *Bapu-ji* took him to a place where a stretch of land separated their fields from the faraway fields westward, he would become quiet and look teary-eyed at the horizon. He would call it "The Border." Juss didn't understand what "The Border" was or what was on the other side. He did not understand why *Bapu-ji's* eyes moistened each time they came there.

"The border is an ignoble outcome of a noble struggle," Bapu Kartar Singh often said. Juss wanted to understand.

Bapu-ji explained to Juss how their ancestors had dedicated their lives to winning freedom from the ninety-eight-year British rule. Many had left the comfort of their homes, their livelihoods and their families to actively engage in the struggle; many were sentenced to death, or to life in prison. Hundreds more were sent away to remote places to die in isolation while their families suffered through anxiety, separation, and poverty.

In 1947, the British left the Indian subcontinent, transferring power to local politicians and splitting the great land of Punjab between two newly formed nations. The western portion, about fifty-seven percent of the land, went to Pakistan, and the eastern portion, about forty-three percent of the land, went to India. The partition

displaced millions of Punjabis along religious lines. Common people didn't have a say in the politics leading to the partition. People who had lived together for millennia were forcibly displaced only because they practiced different faiths even as they spoke the same language and were part of the same Punjabi culture.

More than a million people died in the violence that followed this haphazard partition of the land. Hatred spread by some politicians resulted in looting and killing of innocent people. This mindless violence was further fueled by the anger of displacement, revenge, and greed on both sides. Tens of thousands died of starvation and disease.

During the months of August through October of 1947, forty percent of the Sikh population west of the border had to move to join the other sixty percent on the Indian side. Close to five percent of the total Sikh population is estimated to have vanished in the resulting violence. Likewise, countless Muslims and Hindus were also displaced, and many lost their lives. It was a no-win situation for the common people on either side. In fact, independence pushed Punjab back economically, socially, educationally, and intellectually by decades. The loss of life and the separation from the homeland caused a wound that would never heal.

Village Khalra was half Muslim and half Sikh at the time of partition. At one moment, residents were told that they were going to join Pakistan, and at the next, India. They lived through a long period of uncertainty not knowing which families would be forced out. Such was the case for thousands of residents of villages and cities along "The Border." In the end, in August of 1947, Khalra residents suffered the pain of seeing their Muslim friends and neighbors depart forever.

Bapu-ji explained to Juss that he often came to this place in the hope that he might catch sight of his friends on the other side of "The Border." Sometimes, Juss and *Bapu-ji* would see a few people far, far away, waving at them. They, too, would raise their arms and cry out with joy. The desolate stretch of land between them would come alive for a few moments before returning to an eerie silence.

Juss wondered if the border meant anything to the sun, the moon, the waters, the birds, and the air. Surely it did not, he thought, as the sun rises in the east and sets in the west of Punjab, and the birds fly across freely, too.

Juss and *Bapu-ji* hoped that one day "The Border" would stop separating the people as well.

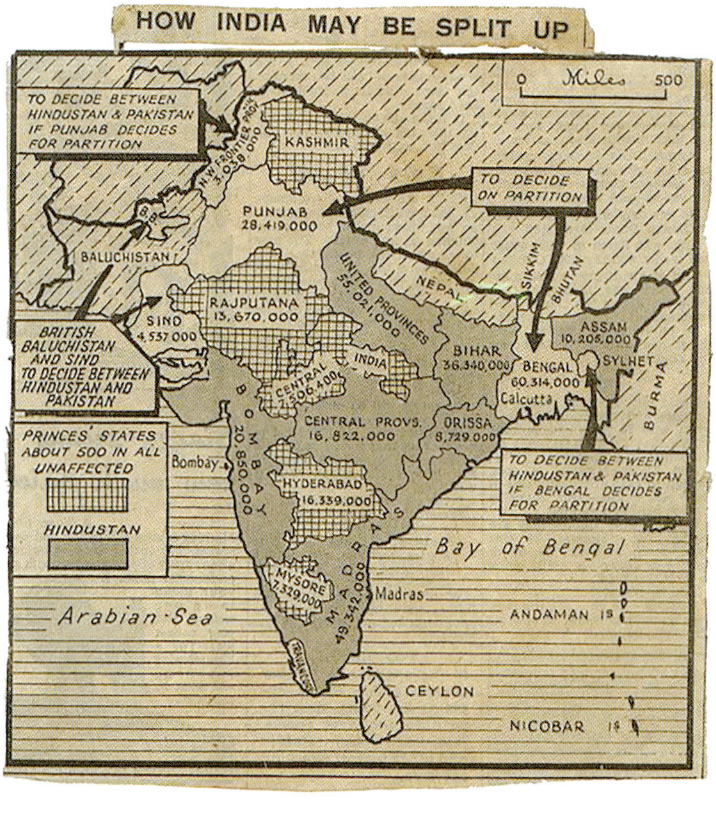

Map speculating on a possible division of India - The Daily Herald, June 4, 1947 National Archives U.K.

PARTITION

WH Auden

Unbiased at least he was when he arrived on his mission,
Having never set eyes on the land he was called to partition
Between two peoples fanatically at odds,
With their different diets and incompatible gods.
"Time," they had briefed him in London, "is short. It's too late
For mutual reconciliation or rational debate:
The only solution now lies in separation.
The Viceroy thinks, as you will see from his letter,
That the less you are seen in his company the better,
So we've arranged to provide you with other accommodation.
We can give you four judges, two Moslem and two Hindu,
To consult with, but the final decision must rest with you."

Shut up in a lonely mansion, with police night and day
Patrolling the gardens to keep the assassins away,
He got down to work, to the task of settling the fate
Of millions. The maps at his disposal were out of date
And the Census Returns almost certainly incorrect,
But there was no time to check them, no time to inspect
Contested areas. The weather was frightfully hot,
And a bout of dysentery kept him constantly on the trot,
But in seven weeks it was done, the frontiers decided,
A continent for better or worse divided.

The next day he sailed for England, where he could quickly forget
The case, as a good lawyer must. Return he would not,
Afraid, as he told his Club, that he might get shot.

(1966)

Sikhs migrating to India after the partition, 1947 - Margaret Bourke-White / Time Life Pictures

The poem is about Sir Cyril Radcliffe, a British Barrister who, as chairman of two boundary commissions including four Judges – two representing the Congress Party and the other two the Muslim League, was responsible for drawing the borders for the new nations of Pakistan and India, in a way that would leave as many Hindus and Sikhs in India and Muslims in Pakistan as possible. He reached Delhi on July 8, 1947 and took five weeks to draw a red line of Pakistan's border – the Radcliffe Line. Partition along the Radcliffe Line led to some 14 million people, roughly seven million from each side, fleeing across the border when they discovered the new boundaries left them in the "wrong" country. Resulting violence killed one million people. After seeing the mayhem occurring on both sides of the boundary, Radcliffe refused his salary of 40,000 rupees (then 3,000 pounds), burnt his papers, and left once and for all.

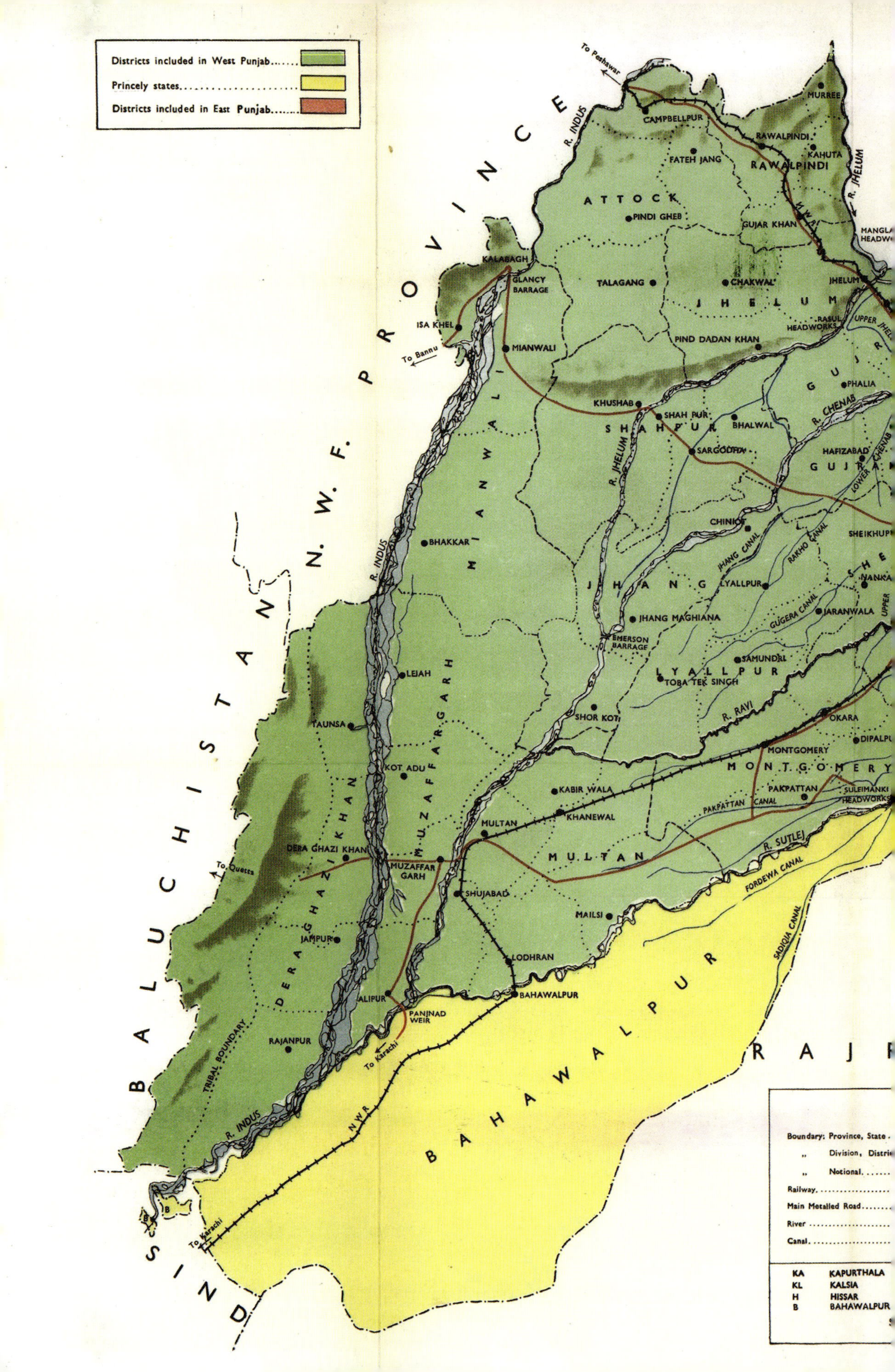

Districts included in West Punjab
Princely states
Districts included in East Punjab
N. W. F. PROVINCE
BALUCHISTAN
SIND
To Peshawar
R. INDUS
CAMPBELLPUR
MURREE
RAWALPINDI
KAHUTA
RAWALPINDI
R. JHELUM
FATEH JANG
ATTOCK
PINDI GHEB
GUJAR KHAN
MANGLA HEADW
KALABAGH
GLANCY BARRAGE
TALAGANG
CHAKWAL
JHELUM
J H E L U M
RASUL HEADWORKS
UPPER JHEL
ISA KHEL
To Bannu
MIANWALI
PIND DADAN KHAN
PHALIA
KHUSHAB
SHAH PUR
BHALWAL
R. CHENAB
S H A H P U R
SARGODHA
HAFIZABAD
R. JHELUM
LOWER CHENAB
M I A N W A L I
CHINIOT
SHEIKHUP
BHAKKAR
JHANG CANAL
RAKHO CANAL
R. INDUS
J H A N G
LYALLPUR
NANKA
JHANG MAGHIANA
GUGERA CANAL
JARANWALA
UPPER
EMERSON BARRAGE
SAMUNDRI
LEIAH
L Y A L L P U R
TOBA TEK SINGH
TAUNSA
SHOR KOT
R. RAVI
OKARA
DIPALPU
MONTGOMERY
M O N T G O M E R Y
KOT ADU
KABIR WALA
PAKPATTAN
SULEIMANKI HEADWORKS
PAKPATTAN CANAL
KHANEWAL
MULTAN
M U Z A F F A R G A R H
D E R A G H A Z I K H A N
DERA GHAZI KHAN
To Quetta
MUZAFFAR GARH
M U L T A N
R. SUTLEJ
FORDEWA CANAL
SHUJABAD
MAILSI
SADIQIA CANAL
JAMPUR
LODHRAN
ALIPUR
BAHAWALPUR
PANJNAD WEIR
To Karachi
RAJANPUR
TRIBAL BOUNDARY
R. INDUS
NWR
B A H A W A L P U R
R A J
To Karachi
B
Boundary: Province, State
Division, Distri
Notional
Railway
Main Metalled Road
River
Canal
KA KAPURTHALA
KL KALSIA
H HISSAR
B BAHAWALPUR

MAP OF THE UNITED PUNJAB BEFORE PARTITION SHOWING THE NOTIONAL BOUNDARY UNDER THE PARTITION PLAN OF 3rd JUNE 1947

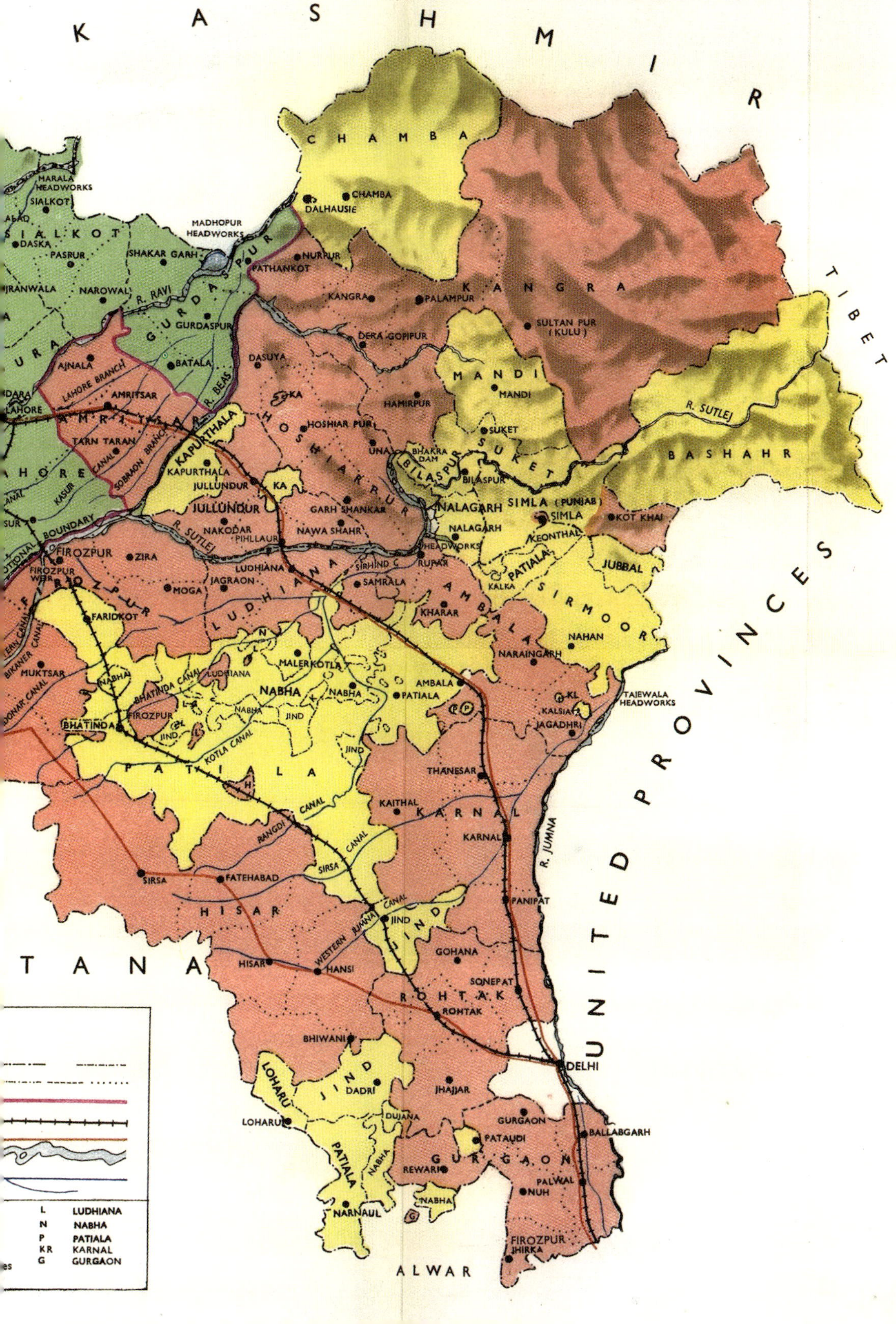

The Legacy

One day, Juss wondered if a hero had ever been born in their own village of Khalra. So he asked *Bapu-ji* about it. He couldn't hold back his excitement when he learned that not just one, but quite a few heroes had been born in the very home in which he lived.

That very day, *Bapu-ji* took Juss to a monument in the village that commemorated the life of Sardar Soora Singh, and he told Juss the army leader's story and that of his commander, Banda Singh Bahadar.

In the year 1708, Banda Singh Bahadar, a Khalsa military general, pledged to punish the cruel ruler of Sirhind, Wazir Khan, who had murdered the young sons and the mother of Guru Gobind Singh, as well as numerous other Sikhs. As Banda Singh marched to Punjab from Southern India, he led a peasant uprising and abolished the *Zamindari* system of land ownership by the aristocrats, granting property rights to the tillers of the land. Before this uprising, the peasants were exploited and kept in poverty, generation after generation. Under Banda Singh's leadership, the peasantry turned into an army that marched on to defeat the Mughal empire. With the power of the people backing him, he successfully ousted the Mughal rulers from Punjab and many parts of Northern India, declared sovereignty, and chose Lohgarh, presently in the Yamunanagar district of Haryana, as his capital city.

Sardar Soora Singh, to whom the monument was dedicated, led one of the army contingents of Banda Singh's. In 1716, Banda Singh and thousands in the Khalsa army were captured, taken to

LAHORE
ਲਾਹੌਰ

Delhi, and martyred. Sardar Soora Singh continued to fight the oppressors, inspiring the common man to rise up against tyranny, and he eventually died fighting Zakariya Khan's forces in village Waañ in 1726. He heroically gave his life as a defiant soldier standing true to his leader and for the right of people to practice their faith.

Juss was a descendent of Soora Singh who had been born in his very home.

Bapu-ji explained that because Khalra was close to Lahore, time and again in the Mughal period, the Sikhs from their village had fought against the repressive rulers from Lahore who were bent on eliminating them. For centuries, Sikhs had provided great resistance defending the right to practice one's own faith and championing equality for all people. Juss was a descendent of some of these warriors. Hearing their stories, Juss felt himself grow taller, more inspired than ever to do great things when he grew up and to add to the legacy of his family and the village.

Bapu-ji promised another story after dinner, that of a great man who was also born in that very home not too long ago – Juss's own grandfather, the father of *Bapu-ji*. As Juss heard this, his eyes opened wide and his heart thumped. He had always wondered why his grandfather was not around. He had heard many stories from the neighbors, in bits and pieces. He was curious to know the truth, but he waited patiently for the day when his father would tell him more.

Finally, that day came.

In the evening after dinner, under the light of a lantern, *Bapu-ji* gathered all his children, opened their *Sandook*, a handcrafted wooden chest that stored special artifacts, and took out a bundle of papers carefully wrapped in a cloth. Among the pictures, letters and newspaper clippings rested a handwritten letter in a postal envelope from Shanghai, China. Sent in 1951, it was the last letter from Harnam Singh Khalra, Jaswant's grandfather, a *Ghadar* Party leader.

"I was about nine years old when he left for Shanghai in 1925. When we left to see him off at the Lahore railway station on a Tonga,* he made me promise to do my *Paath* every day. I have always kept that promise," said *Bapu-ji*, as his eyes reflected the light of the lamp. Awestruck, his senses fully awake, Juss listened attentively, gently touching the letter, even as the other children were ready to fall asleep. *Bapu-ji* continued the story.

Juss's grandfather, Harnam Singh, first joined the British army when Punjab was under the British *Raj*, but soon left because he began to realize that his people needed to be free; serving the British army was not going to help the cause of sovereignty. He made his way to Shanghai via Hong Kong and Burma in order to further the revolutionary movement for freedom. This rebellion for the independence of India was mostly being spearheaded by the Punjabis from abroad as a part of an organized initiative called the *Ghadar* movement that began in the United States of America in 1913. Shanghai and Hong Kong served as the main centers of the *Ghadar* Party in the East. Thousands of Punjabis, mainly the Sikhs who were settled there by the British to work for the police forces in the mid-1800s, had now started to organize for the cause of freedom.

Tonga: Horse-drawn carriage

Paath: Reading from the holy scriptures

On his way, Harnam Singh met Gurdit Singh, a businessman from Singapore influenced by the *Ghadar* movement. Gurdit Singh yearned for the Indian subcontinent to be free from British rule. He wanted to gather like-minded freedom lovers and travel to Canada to expose them to a free country.

He said, "The visions of men are widened by travel, and contacts with citizens of a free country will infuse a spirit of independence and foster yearnings for freedom in the minds of the emasculated subjects of alien rule."

Since Canada was part of the British Empire, and the Punjabis were also British subjects, they believed that immigrating to Canada and working there would not be an issue.

On April 4, 1914, under the leadership of Gurdit Singh, they sailed on the Japanese steamship Komagata Maru that carried 376 Punjabis to Port Vancouver in Canada. However, as they reached the port on May 23, after a fifty-day long and arduous journey, they were denied entry into Canada on imperial orders under the pretext of a law that necessitated "continuous journey" from the country of the passenger's birth. Through such exclusionary laws, the Canadian government prevented people of South Asian origin from emigrating to Canada, even as it was welcoming large numbers of white immigrants from Europe.

After enduring two months of isolation, hunger, and sickness, Gurdit Singh and others were forced to return to India. Harnam Singh was amongst them as well. The ship sailed back to Calcultta on July 23, 1914. The government there, too, treated them as political agitators, and upon landing on September 27, 1914, the police arrested the leaders. When they resisted, the police started

VANCOUVER
VICTORIA
YOKOHAMA
KOBE
MOJI
SHANGHAI
HONG KONG
LCUTTA
SINGAPORE
HONG KONG-SHANGHAI-MOJI-KOBE
YOKOHAMA-VICTORIA-VANCOUVER
VANCOUVER-VICTORIA-YOKOHAMA-KOBE
HONG KONG-SINGAPORE-CALCUTTA

firing and killed nineteen passengers. Komagata Maru Memorial at the Budge Budge port in Bengal, India commemorates the lives of those freedom fighters. The Komagata Maru incident was a catalyst for change to Canadian citizenship and immigration laws, and a monument at Coal Harbor, Vancouver, Canada, pays tribute to this contribution of the Punjabi passengers.

Harnam Singh escaped death and immediate arrest but was later arrested in 1915 along with thirteen other *Ghadar* party members, including the party president, Sohan Singh Bhakhna. In the resulting Lahore Conspiracy Case, the Ghadar party was accused of inciting and planning a pan-India mutiny in the army against the British. Harnam Singh was placed under house arrest in his village for eight years. It was during this time in April of 1916 that his son, Kartar Singh, was born.

The April 1919 *Jallianwala Bagh* massacre of innocent men, women, and children by the British in Amritsar left a wound that could only heal by ousting the British from India. After completing his term of house arrest, Juss's grandfather, Harnam Singh returned to Shanghai in 1925, determined to be a part of the freedom movement, yet again.

He never came back home again.

Bapu-ji showed the letter received by post from Shanghai as the last memory of his father. A long silence filled the air.

Bapu-ji then told Juss about Juss's maternal grandfather, Basant Singh, who was also a freedom fighter with the *Ghadar* party in Shanghai. He told him how Basant Singh and Harnam Singh had met in Shanghai, and how they arranged the marriage of their children back home, which they themselves couldn't attend. He also told him about the hardships faced by both of Juss's grandmothers in raising their families as lone mothers with their husbands having left home to join the struggle for freedom, never to return.

By way of his grandfathers' stories, Juss understood the struggles and sacrifices of thousands of such men, women, and children from Punjab – struggles and sacrifices that eventually paved the way for the Indian subcontinent's freedom from the British. Juss could feel the spirits of those who disappeared into oblivion and whose contributions remained untold; he felt them in that very home, in his very village, in his great land of Punjab.

The lantern's flame was starting to flicker. It was time to sleep but Juss kept thinking of both of his grandfathers. He felt as if he had grown older by many years that day. While his chest swelled with pride, his shoulders felt heavy with responsibility.

Sovereignty, justice, and equality… these words had started to mean a great deal to him.

Gurdit Singh (front left) with his son, Balwant Singh, and other passengers aboard Komagata Maru, 1914 - Leonard Frank / Vancouver Public Library

First Steps

Juss had already carried a spark inside for doing great things; hearing about his grandfathers greatly motivated him. From that day forward, he became a bit more serious, a bit more responsible. His appetite for books grew. He never missed an opportunity to read more about the history, ideology, and struggles of revolutionary leaders from the land of Punjab. He learned all he could about the men and women who stood up for their people and fought against the rulers who benefited from enslaving and oppressing the common folk.

He had come to see that even though the subcontinent was finally free from British rule, the new ruling class continued to oppress the poor, the minorities, and those from the lower castes.

Around the same time, Juss also witnessed Punjab's struggle for its right to remain a Punjabi-speaking region and the discrimination it faced in the newly-formed country of India.

When Juss was barely thirteen, the Indian government started a pension for the families of the freedom fighters. Since his grandfather Harnam Singh had been a *Ghadar* party revolutionary, their family was automatically enrolled in the pension. Juss asked his father not to accept the pension as it would be hypocritical to accept money from a government that engaged in the same policies of exploitation, oppression, and discrimination from which freedom had been won in the first place.

In high school, moved by a sense of personal responsibility, Juss took it upon himself to stand up for the oppressed. He could not tolerate injustice towards anyone. As he advocated for those who had been wronged, the clarity of his thoughts and the power of his written and spoken word inspired friends and strangers alike to join him.

On one occasion, Juss learned that the poor grain-packing laborers in his village *Mandi* had been denied wages by the wealthy marketeers. He became very vocal, and along with a group of young boys and girls from Khalra, he launched a protest to protect the rights of the laborers. This eventually led to fair compensation.

From that day onwards, even as a teenager, Jaswant was considered a champion for the underprivileged. He was endearingly called "*Sadda* Leader" by the common people of the village. They went to him when denied fair compensation by the wealthy as they could never gain an audience with the corrupt and exploitative government officials.

Jaswant was starting to act on his belief that by denying the due right to even one man, the right of every man was under threat. This would be the path he would carve for himself, and it was starting to show.

Sadda: Our

Mandi: Market-place

Jaswant Singh's grandfather Harnam Singh,
a Ghadar activist, Shanghai
- Family collection

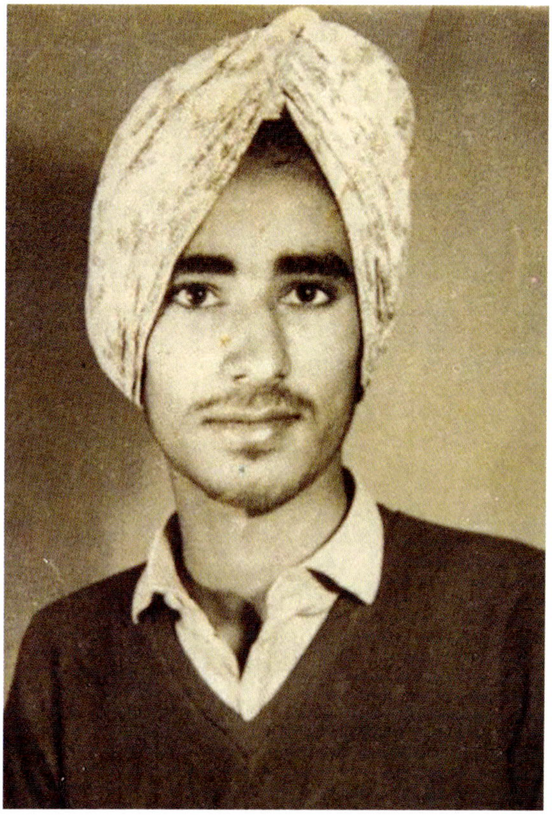

Jaswant Singh at age seventeen
- Family collection

The War

In 1965, India and Pakistan, disgruntled over the division of the partitioned land and by now possessing sufficiently developed military capabilities, engaged in a full-fledged war over the territory of Kashmir. This was already the second war fought between the newly-born countries post-1947. The war soon spread southwards along the border of Punjab. Khalra and hundreds of other border villages were under threat of being bombed and taken over by Pakistan.

Evacuations, blackouts, restrictions on movement, and school and marketplace closures added to the misery of the already difficult lives of millions of people on both sides of the border.

The troops would cut off the crops to ready the area for battle and secure themselves against any infiltrators. This destroyed the farmers' sole source of income. They were never adequately compensated. The population of the border areas was entirely dependent on agriculture and livestock for their survival, as the uncertain security situation discouraged setting up any industrial or commercial activity. Managing animals during evacuation, with fodder crops destroyed, added to the misery. Moving them was usually was not an option, and leaving them behind was emotionally devastating. The town of Khemkaran, located only twenty-five kilometers from Khalra, became an active battle-site between the two countries.

The seventeen-day war resulted in heavy casualties on both sides and involved the largest engagement of armored vehicles and

the largest tank battle since World War II. Hospitals were flooded. Corpses, wounded soldiers and civilians were carried out every day. Everywhere there was chaos, destruction, hunger, and fear. Everywhere there were tears.

The war ended when a ceasefire was declared following a diplomatic intervention by the Soviet Union. After the war, the India-Pakistan border became a Berlin Wall of sorts. Until 1965, visas to visit families across the border were easy, trade ties were better; mail, books, and journals went across easily, and films from both sides were screened across the border. The 1965 war set a tone of greater conflict in the relationship between the two countries.

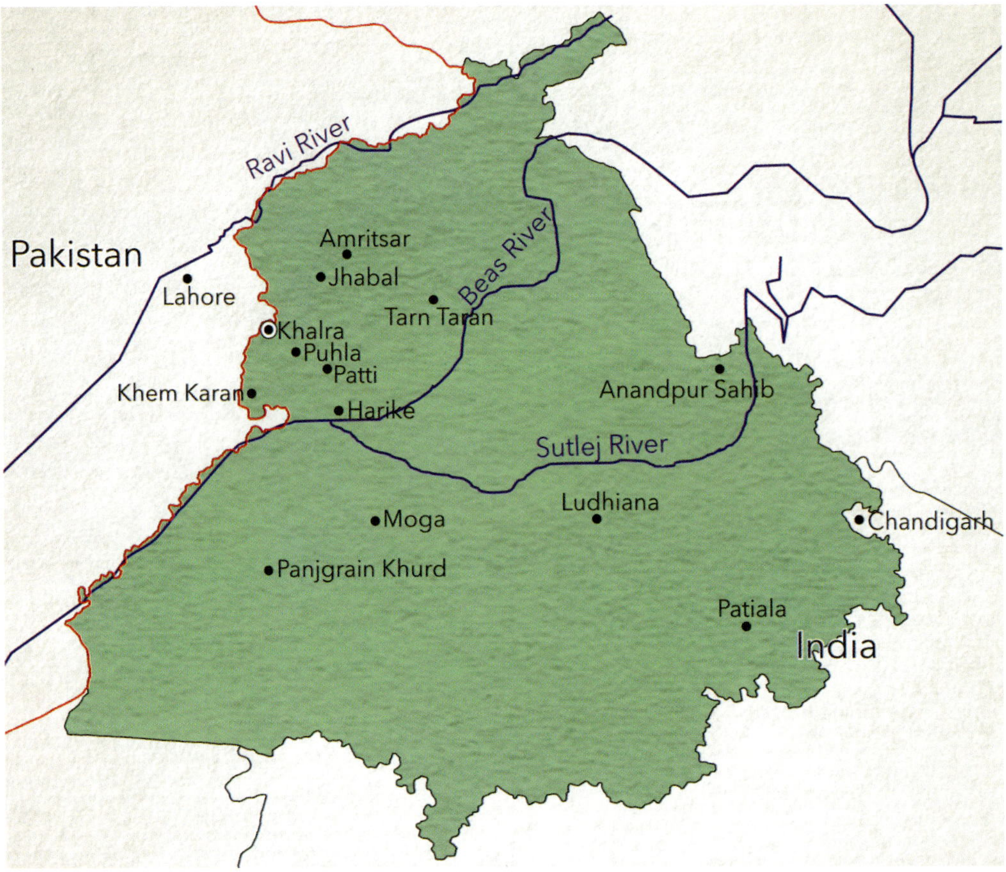

Lieutenant General Harbaksh Singh, General Officer Commanding-in-Chief, Western Command, Indian Army during the Indo-Pakistan War of 1965

Jaswant was saddened by the bloodshed of his people on either side of the border, including those from his own village. He realized more and more that the governments on both sides of the border didn't care about everyday people; they only sought political gain through instilling fear of the "enemy."

Jaswant had learned that the rich and the powerful declared war, but it was the poor who paid the price, the poor who became cannon fodder in the war.

Punjab, Divided Again

In 1966, when Jaswant was only fourteen years of age, the long-standing *Punjabi Sooba* movement that lobbied for Punjab's right to be recognized as a Punjabi-speaking state in India, ended with yet another blow to the land of Punjab. It was a movement in which Punjabis had fought long and hard since the 1950s, and in which thousands of people had been imprisoned. Many lost their lives.

In the 1950s, linguistic groups across India sought statehood, which led to the enactment of the States Reorganization Act in August 1956 – a major reform for the boundaries of India's states and territories that organized them along linguistic lines.

On November 1, 1956, PEPSU – Patiala and East Punjab States Union, a collective of eight Punjabi-speaking Princely States* that had joined India post-independence from the British, was merged into East Punjab. Now, the East Punjab area included the present-day states of Punjab, Haryana, Himachal Pradesh, and Chandigarh. Yet the Indian government kept denying recognition to Punjab as a Punjabi-language state even as it organized other states based on their native languages.

Punjabi, the many thousand-year-old language of the people of Punjab, with many dialects of its own, was dear like a mother to

---

Sooba: State or Province
Princely State: A state under local or indigenous ruler in a subsidiary alliance with the British Raj

Master Tara Singh, freedom fighter and Akali Dal leader, addressing the congregation during his hunger strike for the Punjabi Sooba, Amritsar

Punjabi Sooba agitation supporters protesting, 1955

them. It was now denied the status of the official language in its own land. It was unacceptable that another language, Hindi, would be imposed on the people of Punjab and their own mother tongue would be left to die a painful death.

India's attitude towards the Punjabi language was unacceptable to the Punjabis, particularly to the Sikhs. They identified themselves with the language and its script. They felt especially close to it as the *Guru Granth Sahib*, the Sikh holy scripture, is primarily in the Punjabi language, written in the *Gurmukhi* script. Losing the Punjabi language would mean not only losing the five-thousand-year-old culture of Punjab, but also a great connection to the Sikh faith.

Akali Dal, a Sikh political party in Punjab, realized the threat to the Punjabi language and to the existence of the Sikh faith in the newly formed India posed by the denial of the Punjabi-language state by the Indian government. They launched a movement in protest of the government's discrimination with the demand of *Punjabi Sooba,* a state with Punjabi as its official language. They marched in the thousands, fought for years, courting arrest and giving their lives for the cause.

In 1955, the government made even chanting the words "*Punjabi Sooba*" a punishable offense. In defiance, the *Akalis* started their agitation from *Darbar Sahib* chanting the slogan "*Punjabi Sooba Zindabad.*" On July 4, 1955 police raided the *Darbar Sahib* complex, killing over two hundred protestors, arresting over two

---

Akali Dal: A political party formed in 1920 to give a voice to Sikh issues
Akalis: The members of the Akali Dal party
Zindabad: Long live
Darbar Sahib: The largest and the most eminent center of the Sikh faith, also known as *Harmandir Sahib* or the Golden Temple

thousand, and severely beating and injuring thousands, including women and children.

Eventually, when the central government* agreed to the demands, the Punjab Reorganization Act of 1966 further divided East Punjab into four parts, carving out the new state of Punjab as Punjabi-speaking; and Himachal Pradesh, Haryana, and the Union Territory* of Chandigarh as Hindi-speaking. This was done by unfairly declaring some dialects of Punjabi as Hindi and influencing people

Police raiding Darbar Sahib to crush the Punjabi Sooba agitation, Amritsar, July 4, 1955

Central government: Government of India: The legislative, executive and judicial authority governing the union of twenty eight states and nine union territories, located in New Delhi

Union Territory: An area administered by the central government as opposed to the state government

using those dialects to declare themselves as Hindi-speaking. In the 1951 and the 1961 census, under the influence of leaders who felt threatened by a Sikh-dominated Punjab, the Hindu-majority regions of Punjab recorded Hindi as their mother tongue.

This was yet another betrayal to the land of Punjab and the Punjabi language after the partition of 1947. The Punjab carved in 1966 was now merely fourteen percent of the pre-partition Punjab or thirty-three percent of the post-partition Punjab. Even Punjab's waters were unfairly taken away as the upstream dams controlled by the central government directed waters from the rivers of Punjab outside of their riparian basins* into other states, with no compensation to Punjab in return.

Juss and his family were disenchanted with the Indian government but were even more appalled by the divisive politics and their own people's inability to protect the rights of Punjab. Jaswant wondered if Punjab would ever again see the peaceful days from the times of Maharaja Ranjit Singh,* when the region enjoyed an unparalleled period of prosperity, progress, and the flourishing of education, art, music, and literature.

Juss had already seen so much unrest and yet another dismemberment of his motherland in his life, and he was only a teenager. Little did he know that the years to come would be many times more trying.

Riparian basin: Land along the natural course of a river
Maharaja Ranjit Singh: The pre-British era ruler of Punjab from 1801 – 1839

Kabul
Peshawar
Attock
Is
Rawalpindi
Afghanistan
Khyber
Pakhtunkhwa
Jhelum
Jhelum River
Mianwali
Indus River
Sargodha
Chenab
Gu
Punjab
She
Nankana Sa
Jhang
Faisala
Pakistan
Ravi River
Pakpatt
Multan
Baluchistan
Dera Ghazi Khan
Sutlej River
Bahawalpur
R
Rahimyar Khan
Sindh

East and West Punjab

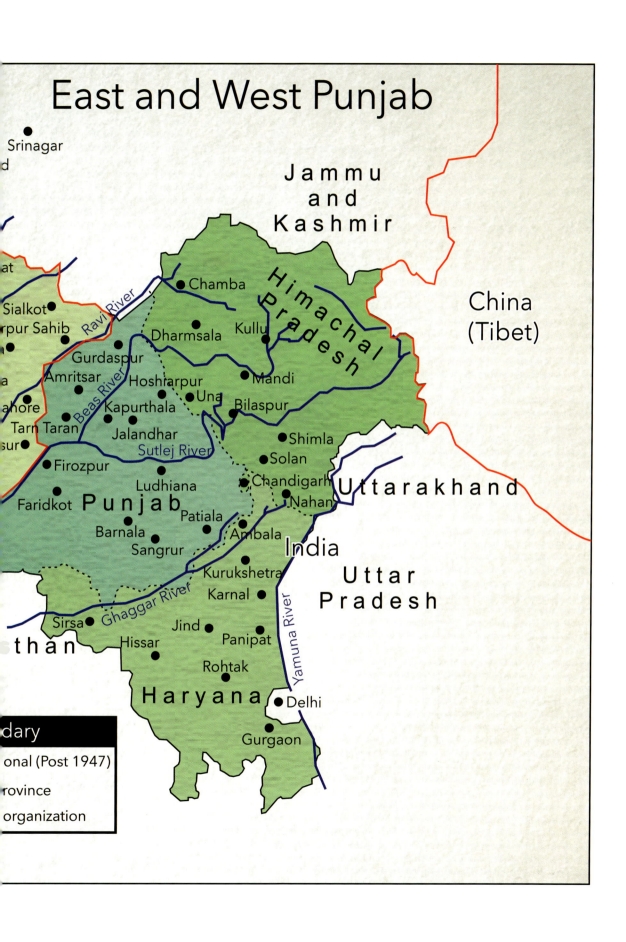

ਅੰਧਕਾਰ ਦੀਪਕ ਪਰਗਾਸੇ॥

In the pitch darkness, a lamp shines forth.

Guru Arjan, SGGS: 287

THE ACTIVIST

The Activist Moves Forward

In 1969, after finishing high school at seventeen years of age, Jaswant enrolled at Baba Buddha College, Bir Sahib, near Jhabal. Jhabal was the birthplace of his childhood hero, Mai Bhago, the legendary female warrior. Being in Jhabal filled Jaswant with awe for his hero and strengthened his already developing desire to look beyond self-interest and stand up for the good of the common people.

Around that time, India's prime minister, Mrs. Indira Gandhi, had initiated a country-wide policy that called for centralization of power that would take much control away from the state governments*. This caused more unrest in Punjab, which had already been stripped of much of its land and its rights over river waters. Many felt that the central government had been unfairly exploiting Punjab's resources without due compensation, and now it was strangling the state even more.

In 1971, under Mrs. Gandhi's orders, India went to war with Pakistan in support of the Bangladeshi independence movement in the then East Pakistan. The war resulted in the creation of the sovereign nation of Bangladesh. Besides the eastern border of India, the war was also fought on the western borders, including Punjab.

Once again, Punjab saw destruction, bloodshed, and chaos. Village Khalra was again evacuated along with all other bordering villages.

State government: The middle tier of the three-tier government setup in India i.e. the central government, the state government, and the local government

ਜਿਥੇ ਲਹੂ ਲੋਕਾਂ ਦਾ ਡੁੱਲ੍ਹ
ਓਥੇ ਲਾਲ ਹਨੇਰੀ ਝੁੱਲ੍ਹ
ਰਾਜ ਭਾਗ ਦਾ ਆਵਾ ਊਤ
ਇਨਕਲਾਬ ਨੇ ਕਰਨਾ ਸੂਤ
ਹੱਕਾਂ ਲਈ ਜੋ ਲੜਦੇ ਲੋਕ
ਜੇਲਾਂ ਤੋਂ ਨਾ ਡਰਦੇ ਲੋਕ
ਜੂਝਦੇ ਜੁਝਾਰ ਲੋਕ
ਫਿੱਟੇ ਮੂੰਹ ਗ਼ਦਾਰ
ਲੋਕ

Through the second war, Jaswant saw the state of people living in constant physical insecurity, putting their lives on hold, seeking shelter during incursions and severe disruptions to education and livelihood. This time around, Jaswant and his brothers decided to stay back and tend to their fields and animals; it was their way of protesting the war.

It bothered Jaswant that India and Pakistan continually went to war with each other rather than resolving their conflicts diplomatically. As a result, the citizens of both nations suffered in poverty. Jaswant also felt that Punjab unnecessarily bore the brunt of these wars both in terms of economic destruction and loss of life. As the Sikhs of Punjab comprised a sizable portion of the Indian Army, most casualties came from their homeland. Jaswant also felt that the people across the border were his own; the idea of brother killing brother appalled him.

Lieutenant General Jagjit Singh Aurora (front center) after liberating Bangladesh, with Pakistani Lieutenant General Amir Abdullah Khan Niazi (right), Dhaka, Bangladesh, December 16, 1971

During this time, Jaswant would engage in anti-war conversations with army personnel and found that most of the troops agreed with him. At one point, someone complained to an army officer that Jaswant was trying to demoralize the army men. Jaswant was summoned by the army officer and warned of serious consequences but it did not deter him. He continued to talk to the troops, inspiring them to be kind to the civilians across the border.

Because of the centralization of powers and the recent wars, Punjabis suffered heavily but were reluctant to speak out against the central government. No act of rebellion against the Indian government, which was fast moving towards a dictatorship model, would go unpunished.

Punjab, however, had a history of standing up against injustice.

There was a socialist movement brewing against the ruling government and the upper class, a movement which sought to alleviate the burden on the poor. A strong believer in the principles of social equality, Jaswant became a natural part of the movement at this young age and joined the left-leaning, socialist, progressive, student groups that were organizing themselves against the government policies that promoted greed, profiteering, and exploitation of the labor class.

While in college, Jaswant organized several protests in support of the rights of the lower economic class. One such protest demanded that public transportation be made affordable for the poor. He also organized a team of students that pushed the government to act against black marketeers of seeds and fertilizers who were exploiting the hard-working farmers.

When Jaswant took a stand on any issue, he did not turn back until he had obtained the desired results. He was clear-headed and did all he could to fully understand a cause before engaging himself. His confidence, leadership, and authority on the issues, and the power of his words began to rattle the government.

At twenty years of age, Jaswant organized and led a protest in which close to ten thousand people demonstrated against the impunity granted to a wealthy businessman accused of killing a youth. Jaswant was arrested by the police. They not only wanted to teach him a lesson but also to subdue his activism and that of other young people like him.

The arrest made Jaswant's parents very nervous. The family sat down to discuss Jaswant's political activism and gently directed him to focus on his studies and career. But it was too late. Jaswant couldn't bring himself to look the other way when he saw injustice around him, especially when people were exploited, harassed or tortured and had no one to stand up for them. It made him especially restless that the ones who were supposed to be protecting and safeguarding the people were the very ones oppressing them.

When Jaswant's brothers reached adulthood, they all moved to Europe in search of a better life. Jaswant had opportunities to leave but chose to stay back to help his parents and to do right by his motherland.

The responsibility he shouldered grew as the conditions around him continued to deteriorate. Every step he took was an answer to the question, "If not I, then who? If not now, then when?"

Jaswant Singh on a college trip to the Taj Mahal - Family collection

Pace Gathers

In 1973, after finishing college at the age of twenty-one, Jaswant moved back to his village to help his family and to continue empowering the people. His experiences made him stronger and more equipped to take on the cause of people's rights. His arrest only made him more resolute. He now knew that he had an element of fearlessness about him which would be a must if he were to continue pursuing the cause of human rights. He knew now that the path of revolution entailed many dangers, and to continue walking this path required a strong character, a solid mind, and most of all, an unbridled passion to serve.

Jaswant had returned with a plan. He established a village library, stocked it with inspiring books to educate people about their rights and to empower them to stand up for themselves and others. He knew that knowledge makes a person unfit to be a slave.

He also opened the Khalra unit office of the newly re-formed organization called *Naujawan Bharat Sabha*. This organization was originally founded by another one of his heroes, the young revolutionary leader, Bhagat Singh, in 1926 at Lahore. Its objective was to seek independence from the British Raj*. It also sought to empower the peasants and the workers to fight for their rights and to have a stake in Indian independence. Jaswant came in contact with this organization while in college and had already established a strong camaraderie with its activists. Now he set about to formally

---

Naujawan Bharat Sabha: Indian Youth Association

British Raj: British Rule

ਜੀਵਨ - ਕਰਤਾਰ ਸਿੰਘ ਸਰਾਭਾ
ਬੱਬਰ ਅਕਾਲੀ ਲਹਿਰ

organize them in the *Majha* area through this office and the library. By now, Jaswant had seen first-hand that the British had left but Bhagat Singh's dream of uplifting the working class was far from being realized. He dreamt of a society where the *Kirti* – the peasants, artisans and laborers – had a voice, and where they did not merely exist to better the lives of others while they, themselves, occupied the bottom rung on the ladder of privilege. Through *Naujawan Bharat Sabha*, Jaswant decided to address the class-based discrimination and to promote fair treatment and wages for the *Kirti*.

Bapu-ji, upon seeing Jaswant's growing political drive, tried to interest his son in extending their farming by adding another agrarian business to it. But Jaswant wanted no part in starting a career that would take him away from his activism.

Jaswant Singh (fourth from left) at the inauguration of the Naujawan Bharat Sabha office, Khalra, 1973 - Family collection

Bapu-ji became quite upset with his son's attitude, and he told Jaswant that it would be hypocritical to talk of empowering the people without being a member of the working class himself. He told his son that he needed to be financially self-sufficient if he were to help others. Jaswant gave his father's counsel some thought, and soon afterward, in 1974, he applied for and was chosen as his village's *Panchayat Secretary,* a public service position appointed by the state government to oversee the *panchayat's* activities, including village development projects.

Through this position, Jaswant ensured that the elected council of his village acted free of corruption, without bias, and spent the allocated funds on genuinely needed development projects. He also used the opportunity to interact with the politically astute in rural communities throughout Punjab. Soon he organized those in positions similar to himself from all over Punjab to work towards the common goal of improving the economic and social conditions of the underprivileged.

Jaswant's integrity, friendly demeanor, and willingness to work hard led to his appointment as the General Secretary of the organization of *Panchayat* Secretaries. With the new organization backing him, he was able to stand up against corruption, discrimination, and exploitation even more fervently than before.

As Jaswant organized the people in his department, senior government officials, some of whom were making handsome money in bribes and under-the-table deals, became very uncomfortable. They warned him to not politicize his official post by making internal

Panchayat: Village council

Jaswant Singh (left) with fellow activists in front of the Shaheed Bhagat Singh Hall, Khalra, 1973 - Family collection

issues a matter of public knowledge and discussions. They asked him to go with the flow or look the other way.

But Jaswant remained undaunted. He led a strike to highlight the issues of rampant corruption and lack of accountability within the department. The big bosses did not take kindly to his defiant stance and began to harass him in various ways. Sometimes he did not receive his salary for months at a stretch. Over time, Jaswant's family began to recognize that the struggle for truth and justice was Jaswant's way of life.

Jaswant was unforgiving of those who stole public money, and he made an example of them. Once, the *Sarpanch* of his village embezzled a large amount of money by falsifying wages paid to

---

Sarpanch: Head of the village council

laborers working on a project. In making up the names of the laborers, he drew from a file which happened to include Jaswant's father's name, Kartar Singh, on it, too. While overseeing this project's files, Jaswant immediately discovered the fraudulent activity, and he investigated and exposed the fraud publicly, greatly embarrassing the *Sarpanch*.

Though the *Sarpanch* begged for forgiveness, Jaswant saw to it that he was removed from his position and prosecuted for his crime. Despite the possibility of dangerous repercussions to himself, Jaswant wanted to set an example for others in power to serve without corruption.

He believed that corruption was like a snowball; once it was set rolling, it went on getting larger and larger. The only way to stop corruption was to nip it in the bud.

Jaswant Singh and fellow activists protesting the Indo-Pakistan wars, advocating a confederation of the two countries - Family collection

The Anandpur Sahib Resolution

After some years of holding the Punjab-wide position of the General Secretary of the *Panchayat* Secretaries association and running the local unit of *Naujawan Bharat Sabha*, Jaswant wanted to collaborate with his other Indian counterparts to further the cause of social justice.

Bapu-ji, upon seeing his son's unrelenting political inclinations, encouraged Jaswant to join one of the major political parties of Punjab, the *Akali Dal* or the Congress Party*. He believed that in order to effect change, Jaswant needed to work from within the establishment. But Jaswant could not reconcile himself with the politics of either party. He viewed their leaders as self-serving opportunists.

To expand his horizons and effect even more change, Jaswant ended up joining a newly reformed leftist political party called the International Democratic Party that advocated non-violent means to end injustice towards the common people. The party was active in Kashmir and in the Punjab region. Its members believed in peace between India and Pakistan and wanted joint governance of Kashmir by the two countries. The conflict over Kashmir had led the two neighboring countries to war more than once.

Meanwhile, the policy of centralizing power between 1967 and 1971 had caused enormous strain in the relationship between the state government of Punjab and the central government.

Congress Party: A major political party in India founded in 1885. It lead the Indian independence movement and formed the first government post-1947 partition

Appendix - I
189
Anandpur Sahib Resolution
Whereas the Sikhs of India are a historically recognised political nation ever since the inauguration of the Order of the Khalsa in the Concluding Year of the 17th Century, and
Whereas this Status of the Sikh nation has been internationally recognised and accepted by major Powers of Europe and Asia
France, England, Italy
ANANDPUR SAHIB
RESOLUTION

The Punjabis felt that they were not able to address poverty, economic development, and class equity fairly because of the central government's control. They felt betrayed as the central government had unfairly taken control of Punjab's river waters, allocating the resource to other states without compensation to Punjab. They also felt that Punjabi farmers, who produced the majority of the grain for the rest of the country, were being denied due compensation for their produce.

The earlier wounds sustained from the central government's resistance to giving Punjabi an official-language status and from truncating Punjab to carve two new states out of it were still fresh. The state government maintained that the Punjabi-speaking areas, including the Union Territory of Chandigarh, had been unfairly cut out of Punjab and must be returned.

The *Akali Dal*, a partner in the coalition government of Punjab, wanted to protect the Sikh faith. Pakistan was formed so the Muslims could practice their faith without the interference of the Hindu majority. Hindus were protected in the new India by virtue of their status as a majority. But the Indian constitution did not give Sikhs their due status as a people belonging to an independent faith. This did not go well with the *Akali Dal*, which wanted the Sikh faith declared as an independent faith with its articles and customs protected.

The *Akali Dal* felt that the central government created hurdles in the Punjab government's functioning and progress. It pushed the state government to take up the issue of its relations with the central government. In October 1973, the working committee of the *Akali Dal* adopted a policy resolution at a conference held at the city of Anandpur that would come to be known as "The Anandpur Sahib

Resolution." The resolution was drafted by the Sikh philosopher, theologian, and writer, Sirdar Kapur Singh, who as an Indian Civil Service (ICS) officer had witnessed first-hand the government's demeaning and discriminatory attitude towards the Sikhs.

It demanded autonomy for the state government from the central government in all areas except defense, foreign relations, currency, and communications. It asked for fair compensation for the state's resources that were controlled by the central government. It also asked for structural arrangements that would give Sikhs a dominant role in the administration of Punjab.

Although Jaswant appreciated the demand for decentralization and fair compensation in return for the use of the state's resources, he was critical of the resolution's language regarding the political dominance of the Sikhs in the state. In his opinion, Sikhs should not conflate the battle for their religious rights with the common political rights of all people.

He believed that the Sikh faith, which had survived centuries of persecution due to commitment of its adherents, could not be endangered because of government policy alone. Thus, he saw no need for the *Akali Dal* to play along the rhetoric of endangered faith, and appear communal. Instead he felt that the *Akali Dal* needed to identify themselves with the cause of minorities all over the country, especially the Muslims and the *Dalits* who had suffered even more from India's ruling class.

He wanted the *Akali Dal* to take the stance of the founding principles of their faith, to stand up against injustice towards anyone, rather

---

Dalit: A class of people considered lower than and outside of the Hindu caste system

than isolating themselves by talking of Sikh rights alone. He believed that the *Akali Dal* was falling for the central government's manipulation by playing the religious card. He said that the injustice of the Indian democracy caused by the Hindu-dominated majority could not be fought by creating a Sikh-dominated majority in the state of Punjab; two wrongs would never make a right.

Jaswant didn't want to create further division along religious lines. Instead, he dreamt of healing the pain caused by the haphazard partition of the country in 1947. He tried to persuade the *Akali Dal* to rise above their limited mindset and consider his proposal of a "confederacy between India and Pakistan," which would mean that both countries would work together politically for the common good of their people, who not only shared the land, water, language, and culture, but had also faced many of the same social, economic, and educational issues.

Jaswant felt that the politics of religious nationalism promoted hatred, and both countries needed to move away from using hate as a political tool. Instead, they should make their politics purposeful and progressive for everyone, including their religious and ethnic minorities. He suggested moving away from repressive centralization towards a framework that could better accommodate regional self-governance safeguarding fundamental rights of the religious and ethnic minorities.

Jaswant believed that progress and peace on the subcontinent could be brought about if the downtrodden and the oppressed, the religious and ethnic minorities in India and Pakistan, came together to rise up against inequality and injustice.

He believed that to be happy, human beings needed to build bridges rather than walls. Walls can turn even a paradise into a prison.

The Emergency

While Jaswant continued to work for the betterment of the common people, the relationship between the state of Punjab and the central government became more and more troublesome. The central government was by now facing nationwide opposition against its repressive policies, with the loudest of the opposition coming from the *Akali Dal* in Punjab.

In June 1975, the Prime Minister of India and the leader of Congress Party, Indira Gandhi, was convicted of election fraud. She proclaimed a national emergency, suspending the Indian constitution to save her government from falling and to curb nationwide agitation against herself. For almost two years, she ruled by suppressing civil liberties, arresting political opponents, imposing press censorship, and banning all political protests.

Even so, the *Akali* leaders in Punjab organized public protests against her dictatorial measures. As a result, the protestors were detained without trial. The government imprisoned over forty thousand *Akalis* (mostly Sikhs) for violating her diktats. The government vilified the Sikh community in the media as troublemakers and separatists. Many Sikhs from village Khalra were arrested as well.

For the first time, Jaswant Singh admired the organizational strength of the *Akali Dal* as they engaged thousands of people to non-violently challenge Indira Gandhi's dictatorship. No other political party in India had been able to match the *Akali Dal*'s performance in defiance against this authoritarian control.

Eventually, the *Janata Party*, an alliance of over a dozen political parties at the national level, including the *Akali Dal*, defeated the Congress party in the elections of March 1977 and formed a government at the center.

In the meanwhile, the *Akali Dal* policy makers put forth a comprehensive version of the Anandpur Sahib Resolution. It was passed on October 28 - 29, 1977, in the general session of the party's meeting at Ludhiana, which was attended by over one hundred thousand people. The resolution opened with the demand for decentralization of powers.

Jaswant hoped that the broad coalition of democratic parties that replaced Indira Gandhi's repressive regime would fulfill its promises. He hoped that it would pursue the cause of decentralization of power, focus on the development of the economically backward, and establish respect for the fundamental human rights of all people. To Jaswant Singh's utter dismay, Morarji Desai, the Prime Minister of the coalition government, announced that he would not agree to any proposal for an amendment in the constitution in the matter of decentralization, deviating from *Janata Party's* earlier stance.

To Jaswant's further disappointment, the *Akali Dal* government in Punjab, with Prakash Singh Badal as the Chief Minister, seemed complicit in this new stance. It did not want to jeopardize its relationship with its coalition partners that now forbade the very words, "autonomy" or "decentralization."

Apparently the *Akali Dal's* desire for power had started to outweigh its resolve to stand up for its principles.

Sikhs who placed themselves at the head of the nation;

Who showed themselves as interpreters of the rights of the people;

Who maintained the struggle between good and evil, between the sovereign will of the people and the divine right of kings, and the opposition of liberty to despotism;

Who avenged the insults, the outrages and slavery of many generations of the past; who liberated their mother country from the yoke of the foreign oppressor;

Who displayed all that was great and noble; who left to the children of this province a heritage unsullied by the presence of any foreign soldier;

Who won for the Punjab the envied title of "the land of soldiers";

Who alone can boast of having erected a "bulwark of defence against foreign aggression," the tide of which had run its prosperous course for the preceding eight hundred years; and to

Whom all other people of Northern India in general and the Punjab in particular, owe a deep debt of gratitude.

Hari Ram Gupta (1902 - 1992)
Renowned Historian

The Provocation

In 1978, when Jaswant was 26 years old, an event took place that was to shake Punjab and change the lives of many young men and women.

On April 13, 1978, one hundred Sikhs decided to peacefully march in protest against a *Sant-Nirankari* convention led by their cult leader, Gurbachan Singh Nirankari. *Sant-Nirankaris* had hurled abuses and insults at the Sikh holy scripture, the *Guru Granth Sahib*, at previously held processions. The heavily armed cult members fired upon the peaceful Sikh protesters. Thirteen Sikhs, including a prominent Sikh leader, Bhai Fauja Singh, were shot dead, and seventy-eight were wounded. All this occurred in Amritsar, the center of the Sikh faith, very near the *Darbar Sahib*, where the Sikhs had been celebrating the festival of Vaisakhi in large numbers. Instead of helping, the police fired tear gas shells at the protesters. This atrocity was clearly supported by the government as no action was taken against the killers and the cult leader.

On September 25, 1978, a second case of violence occurred amid another peaceful Sikh protest against the same cult in Kanpur; it took a dozen lives and injured over seventy Sikhs, and this time the Sikhs were brought down by police bullets. This act also went unpunished by the Indian government.

The whole of Punjab was shocked, and the Sikhs were extremely hurt and angry. Any assault on the *Guru Granth Sahib* was an

---

Sant-Nirankari: A dissident cult that broke away from the Sikh faith

ਵਾਹਿਗੁਰੂ
ਵਾਹਿਗੁਰੂ
WAHEGURU
WAHEGURU
ਵਾਹਿਗੁਰੂ
WAHEGURU
ਵਾਹਿਗੁਰੂ
ਵਾਹਿਗੁਰੂ
WAHEGURU
WAHEGURU
ਵਾਹਿਗੁਰੂ
WAHEGURU

assault on their identity and their faith; an act insulting their very existence. These incidents sent a clear message that the Sikhs could not even peacefully protest attacks on their own faith; there was no protection for the Sikh faith in India.

All of Jaswant's family members were devout Sikhs who held the *Guru Granth Sahib's* honor higher than their own lives. Everyone in the family read from the holy scriptures daily and with much reverence. They also read the entire *Granth Sahib* every year on the occasion of Diwali, a centuries-old family tradition. Jaswant himself was very connected to *Gurbani* – the hymns from the *Guru Granth Sahib.* Like Sikhs all over the world, Jaswant and his family were deeply agonized by the insults and killings of the protesting Sikhs.

The events of April and September of 1978 had a profound effect upon Jaswant. He began to understand and appreciate the need to safeguard the Sikh faith as enunciated in the Anandpur Sahib Resolution. He developed a respect for the struggle to secure due rights for the Sikhs along with the rights of Punjab as promised by the Indian government in 1947. The struggle also gained the sympathy and ideological backing of thousands of Punjabi youth who were originally part of the leftist movement.

They had come to realize that Punjab was denied its due share because most of its citizens practiced the Sikh faith, and if equality and justice had a place in Punjab, this was the first battle to fight.

Mass cremation of the thirteen Sikhs killed at the protest against the Sant-Nirkari cult leader, Amritsar, April 13, 1978

The Partner

In 1979, as a part of his activism and work with Punjab Student Union in Khalsa College, Amritsar, Jaswant met a young student leader, some eight years younger, named Gurbhajan Singh, lovingly called Bhej. Juss and Bhej clicked right away and became close, more like brothers than friends. They organized meetings and inspired students to challenge the injustice they saw around them.

Bhej had an older sister named Paramjit Kaur who was a member of a socialist student union in her own college. She had a degree in Punjabi language from the Punjabi University, Patiala, and was now enrolled in the study of Library Sciences at the Guru Nanak Dev University in Amritsar. Bhej thought that Paramjit and Jaswant would make a wonderful couple and mentioned this to both several times. Before they could meet, however, Bhej met with a fatal accident. Before he passed away, he reiterated to his family and to both Jaswant and Paramjit his wish for them to be married. Everyone honored Bhej's final wishes.

In 1981, at the age of twenty-nine, Jaswant Singh married Paramjit Kaur, twenty-seven, of village Panjgarai Khurd. Paramjit began working as a teacher in the nearby village of Puhla. Jaswant assisted his father. He also continued his job as the *Panchayat* Secretary, presiding over its Punjab-wide organization, and he continued his activism with the *Naujawan Bharat Sabha*. These responsibilities kept Jaswant busy, and sometimes he would have to leave for days at a time, whereupon Paramjit would readily take on the village responsibilities in his absence.

Bhej had been right. Jaswant and Paramjit became a team with a common purpose in life, to make things better for their beloved land and its people. Jaswant felt that his strength had doubled. Paramjit, too, was happy to contribute and learn from their "leader."

Memorial service of Gurbhajan Singh at Khalsa College, Amritsar, 1981 - Family collection

Jaswant Singh (left) with Gurbhajan Singh, 1981 - Family collection

Anand Karaj (wedding ceremony) of Jaswant Singh and Paramjit Kaur, Panjgrain Khurd, District Moga, 1981 - Family collection

The Struggle

While the couple lived in Khalra, Punjab's struggle against the central government for its rights was gaining momentum. This struggle for the rights of all of Punjab came to be known as the Sikh Struggle Movement, as Sikhs were at its forefront.

Leaders of the movement asked that the demands in the Anandpur Sahib Resolution be fulfilled, allowing the state control of its own resources without any undue interference from the central government.

The main demand in the resolution sought control of Punjab's river waters. By commandeering seventy-five percent of Punjab's water and directing it via canals to other states, the government of India was violating international riparian covenants which gave the first right of the river water to the people who lived in its basin. This forced Punjab, an agrarian economy, to irrigate eighty-five percent of its fields from underground aquifers, depleting the emergency reserves. Punjab, the land of five rivers, was being deprived of its own precious resources and being pushed to the verge of desertification. It was also forced to use oil and electricity for extracting underground water which it had to either purchase or produce on its own, causing a great environmental, social, and economic crisis for its people. Farming was becoming unviable, creating debt for farmers that they were unable to repay.

The resolution also asked for the return of the Punjabi-speaking territories that were wrongly declared as Hindi-speaking in 1966. This included the Union Territory of Chandigarh which had been

OWNERSHIP OF NATURAL RESOURCES
ECONOMIC RIGHTS
ਜਾਬੀ ਇਲਾਕਿਆਂ ਦੀ ਵਾਪਸੀ
ਮਾਂ-ਬੋਲੀ
ਸਿੱਖ ਹਸਤੀ
SIKH IDENTITY
SUSTAINABLE AGRICULTURE
ਪਾਣੀ
WATER
ਸਿਆਸੀ ਹੱਕ
RN OF PUNJABI SPEAKING AREAS
ਆਰਥਿਕ ਹੱਕ
ENVIROMENTAL PROTECTION
SOCIAL DEVELOPMENT
ਲਾਹੇਵੰਦ ਖੇਤੀਬਾੜੀ
MOTHER-TONGUE
ਵਾਤਾਵਰਨ ਦੀ ਰਾਖੀ
AUTONOMY
ਸਮਾਜਿਕ ਵਿਕਾਸ
ਦਮੁਖਤਿਆਰੀ
POLITICAL RIGHTS
ਕੁਦਰਤੀ ਸੋਮਿਆਂ ਦੀ ਮਾਲਕੀ
ANANDPUR IS FAR

created post-partition to be the new capital of East Punjab after the previous capital of Lahore became part of West Punjab in Pakistan. Chandigarh was a planned city carved by demolishing about fifty Puadhi* speaking villages of Punjab, displacing the natives and changing the linguistic, religious, and cultural demography of the area.

The Anandpur Sahib Resolution, *inter alia,* also sought recognition of the Sikh faith as an independent faith in the constitution of India and protection for the Sikh articles of faith.

Meanwhile, Indira Gandhi won the 1980 elections and again became the Prime Minister. She was determined to teach the Sikhs and particularly *Akali Dal* a lesson for their resistance during her previous regime. She held them responsible for ousting her from power in the past.

The unwillingness of the government to punish the perpetrators of the Sikh killings in the two Sikh-Nirankari clashes of 1978 resulted in the assassination of the cult leader, Gurbachan Singh Nirankari. On April 24, 1980, a devout Sikh named Ranjit Singh, upset at the cult-leader's continuous insults, government backing, and protection; shot him dead at his Delhi headquarters. Although Ranjit Singh managed to escape initially, he surrendered in 1983 and was sentenced to life in prison. The Congress Party used this episode to isolate the *Akali Dal* as a Sikh extremist party by providing false media accounts of the clashes and painting the Sikhs as terrorists backed by Jarnail Singh Bhindrawale.

Puadhi: One of the close to twenty-five major dialects of the Punjabi language
Sant: Revered, spiritually enlightened

Jarnail Singh Bhindrawale had been a Sikh spiritual preacher *par excellence,* with unparalleled charisma and a great following. He was the then head of the *Damdami Taksal,* a leading Sikh seminary dating back to the time of the tenth Guru of the Sikhs, Guru Gobind Singh. He was determined to fight the plagues of alcoholism, forced dowry, and the sexual exploitation of women, as well as other ethical issues that he believed were destroying the future of Punjab. He did so by connecting Sikhs to their prescribed discipline, which required them to keep their Sikh identity, to forsake all addictions including alcohol, and to honor women. He also inspired Sikhs to be ready to defend their faith from internal as well as external attacks.

Jarnail Singh Bhindrawale was concerned that government policies such as stripping Punjab of its waters, price-control of agricultural products adversely affecting the farmers, and the promotion of alcohol were weakening the economic, social and moral fabric of Punjab. He considered the government backing of various anti-Sikh cults as a direct attack on the Sikh faith.

Jarnail Singh Bhindrawale was critical of the *Akali Dal* for dragging its feet on the Sikh Struggle Movement. He spoke in straightforward language and in a manner that appealed to the people of the rural areas. He had an impeccable reputation because he courageously spoke the truth. His integrity could not be questioned or bought by the government, despite their efforts. In a few short years and at a young age, he came to be venerated by the masses who started to affectionately address him as "*Sant*" Bhindrawale.

Thus he had garnered much support, including that of some radical Sikh youth frustrated by the state of affairs and ready to take up arms to defend their rights. Around that time, several political assassinations took place, and reports that they were carried out by armed Sikhs rattled Punjab.

The ruling Congress Party now had all the ammunition they needed to use the Sikh cause to their political advantage. They alleged that *Sant* Bhindrawale was behind the killing of Hindus in Punjab. Reportedly, these killings were often orchestrated by the government itself to create an environment of hate and fear and to vilify *Sant* Bhindrawale in the media.

Dialogue on the central government-state relationship with Punjab had no chance of revival now. Indira Gandhi used the environment in Punjab to create the semblance of a Hindu-Sikh rift where there was none. By painting Sikhs as terrorists and separatists who roamed Punjab killing innocents, she was able to turn the mainstream urban population against the Sikh political party, the *Akali Dal*.

In May 1980, the Congress Party defeated the *Akali Dal* in the State Assembly elections and formed a government in Punjab. With the Congress Party in power in both the central and local state government, propaganda against the Sikhs escalated. *Sant* Bhindrawale, who, like the *Akali Dal,* was an ardent supporter of the Anandpur Sahib Resolution, demanded its implementation. He quickly emerged as the face of the struggle. Villagers turned out in the thousands to listen to *Sant* Bhindrawale and to pledge their support to him.

On September 9, 1981, Jagat Narain, an influential political leader, and owner of the media group, *Hind Samachar*, was gunned down by unknown Sikhs. Jagat Narain was instrumental in the trifurcation of Punjab by encouraging the Hindus of Punjab to declare Hindi as their mother tongue. Through his newspapers, he was believed to be involved in painting the Anandpur Sahib Resolution as anti-Hindu, sectarian, and secessionist, rather than depicting it as the economic and social reform that it was. This promoted the

semblance of a Hindu-Sikh rift, which paved the way for the central government to crush the Sikh Struggle. He was a key witness in the Sikh-Nirankari clashes and had testified against the Sikhs. His insulting remarks on Guru Gobind Singh, the the tenth Guru of the Sikhs, was the final straw.

On September 20, 1981, *Sant* Bhindrawale was arrested on charges of terrorism by the government for ordering the assassination of Jagat Narain. The whole of Punjab exploded in anger opposing this arrest. Sikhs in great numbers protested in Mehta Chowk, home of *DamDami Taksal*, where *Sant* Bhindrawale was arrested. The police gunned down eleven protestors.

On September 29, 1981, five members of *Dal Khalsa*, a Sikh organization, hijacked an Indian Airlines flight carrying 111 passengers from Srinagar to Delhi and directed it to Lahore. They demanded the release of *Sant* Bhindrawale. All passengers and the flight crew were released unharmed by the hijackers before they themselves surrendered.

A month after *Sant* Bhindrawale's arrest, the government determined that there was no evidence against him on any charges, and he was acquitted on October 15, 1981. In 1982, *Sant* Bhindrawale formally launched the *Dharam Yudh Morcha*, the movement against state injustice. Thousands of Sikhs joined him, supported his demands, and peacefully protested against the government. By now the *Akali Dal* had come to fully support the *Dharam Yudh Morcha*, as well. Sikhs in large numbers kept courting arrest during the protests.

Dal Khalsa: A Sikh political organization formed in 1978 with the objective of Sikh sovereignty

Dharam Yudh Morcha: The movement for protection of faith

At the same time, frustrated by the government's adamant refusal to accede to their demands, the militant group *Babbar Khalsa* launched an armed struggle for an independent nation, Khalistan.* They contended that India was protecting only the majority Hindus, and the rights of the Sikhs on the subcontinent could only be safeguarded in a nation-state governed by Sikhs. The *Dal Khalsa*, too, endorsed the idea of Khalistan, albeit through peaceful means.

As tensions mounted, the government increasingly portrayed the Sikhs as violent and unruly people who presented a threat to ordinary Indians and to the integrity of India. *Sant* Bhindrawale was portrayed by the media as the number-one enemy of India who was spewing hatred towards Hindus. His speeches were banned in print and on electronic media so that the masses would not have access to the complete truth. Newspapers often carried mistranslated snippets of his speeches that worked to further the propaganda.

In the name of national security, the central government set the stage to garner the sympathy and support of mainstream Indians to create leverage in the upcoming elections. At the same time, under the guise of curbing terrorism, the government gave a free hand to the Punjab Police and the security forces. As a result, devout Sikhs were harassed and tortured. Between 1981 and 1984, hundreds were tortured in police custody while many were murdered in "staged encounters."* Thousands were arrested for demanding their civil rights.

In November of 1982, India hosted the Asian Games in New Delhi. The *Akali Dal* called for peaceful protests to bring the plight of

---

Khalistan: Sovereign land of the Khalsa

Staged encounters: Staging of fake encounters by the police or security forces to cover up custodial killings, or to falsely portray the suspect as a militant attacking the forces

Punjab to the world media. The government arrested thousands of Sikhs, including *Akali Dal* leaders and Punjab state legislators, to keep them from organizing at any level.

Police in Haryana, the state between Punjab and Delhi, turned back any groups of Sikhs heading towards the capital. They searched vehicles at the checkpoints guarding the main entrances to the capital. Sikhs were profiled, singled out, harassed, and turned back from attending the games even as they represented a good percentage of India's sports teams. Prominent military figures, such as retired Marshal of the Indian Air Force, Arjan Singh, who served as Third Chief of the Air Staff, and Lieutenant General Jagjit Singh Arora, who was the General Officer Commanding-in-Chief in the 1971 Bangladesh war, were mistreated as well. Sikhs that were not even a part of the *Akali* movement felt alienated and humiliated by these actions.

In 1983, Indira Gandhi imposed President's Rule, sending home the elected government of Punjab, and Punjab fell under the tight grip of the central government.

While Jaswant and Paramjit continued to work on issues of social justice, they were suddenly flooded by human rights abuse cases wherein common people suffering at the hands of the police or the militants came to them for help. There were cases of illegal detentions, kidnappings, and disappearances for which no one knew to whom they could turn for redress.

As much as the excesses of the police bothered Jaswant, so did the militant stance of the Sikh radicals. He was as hurt by the killing of the Hindus as he was by the murder of Sikhs. He believed that violence was no solution to any issue in Punjab.

He could see that extremism and the easy flow of arms that Punjab was witnessing was an ominous sign of the times to come.

Sirdar Kapur Singh (left) with Sant Jarnail Singh in Darbar Sahib Complex, 1984 - Satpal Danish

ਏਤੀ ਮਾਰ ਪਈ ਕਰਲਾਣੇ ਤੈਂ ਕੀ ਦਰਦੁ ਨ ਆਇਆ॥

There was so much slaughter that the people screamed.
Didn't You feel compassion, O Lord?

Guru Baba Nanak, SGGS: 360

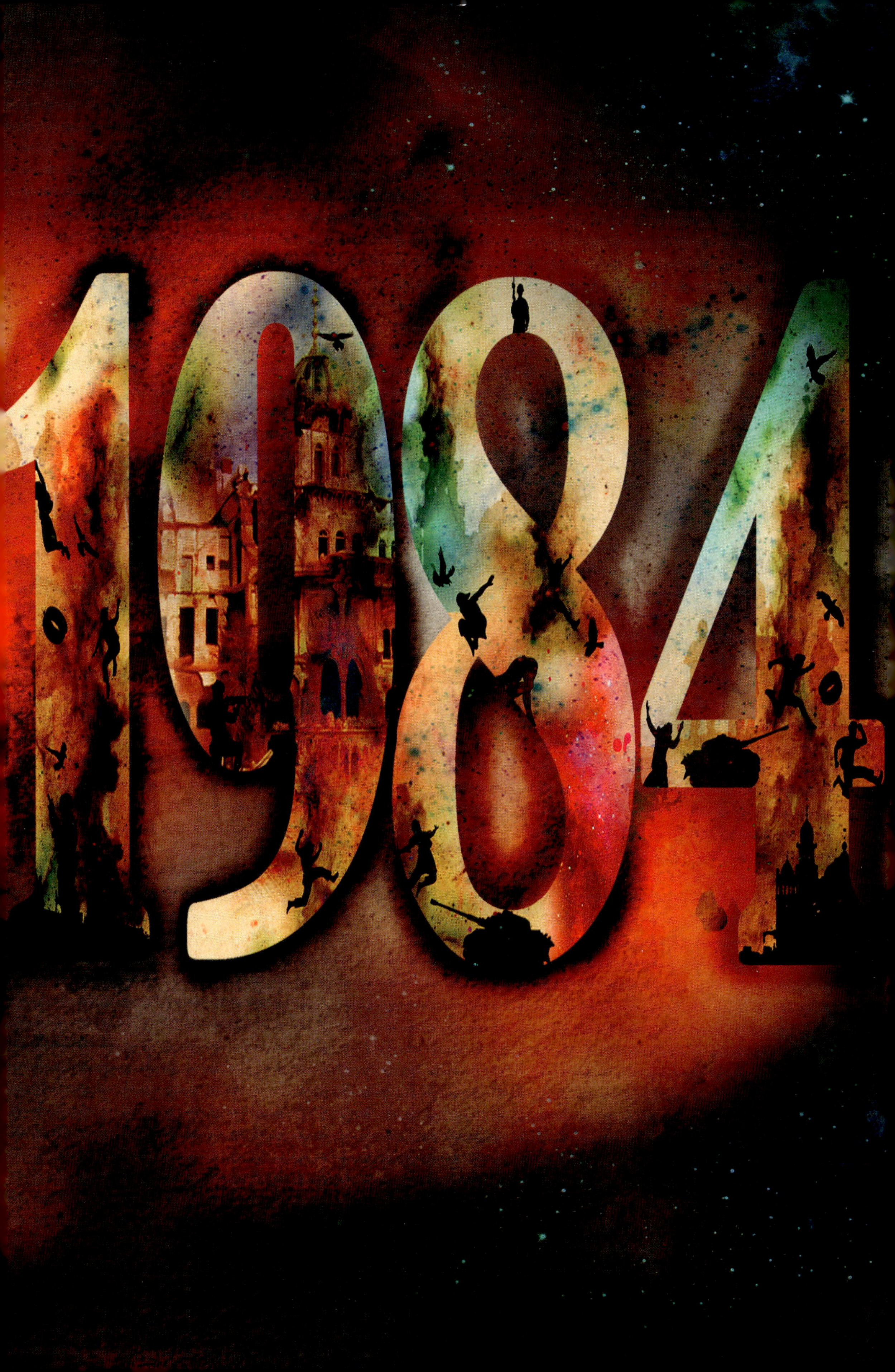
1984

Dark Clouds Gather

Three short years after their marriage, two events in 1984 would come to define Jaswant's and Paramjit's destiny, as they would for thousands of other Sikhs, young, old or newly born, men or women, whether they lived in Punjab, in India, or in the diaspora.

On May 24, 1984, the *Akali Dal* announced that as of June 3, they would intensify their movement against the central government. They decided to block the transfer of Punjab's grains to other states and withhold all taxes due to the government. They planned for their members to court arrest until the central government agreed to the demands of Anandpur Sahib Resolution, or at least, agreed to begin a dialogue. Many *Akali* volunteers mobilized towards Amritsar. Simultaneously, between May 25 and May 31, the government deployed about 100,000 troops throughout Punjab and encircled forty historical and popular gurdwaras in the state, including the *Darbar Sahib*, Amritsar, the largest and most prominent Sikh center of worship in the world.

The Armed Forces (Punjab and Chandigarh) Special Powers Act (AFSPA), 1983, a law that granted special powers to the Indian Armed Forces to maintain public order in areas of disturbance, empowered security forces to search any premises and to arrest people without a warrant. It also allowed security forces to use deadly force on suspected terrorists and granted prosecutorial impunity to the officials for any action taken while enforcing the AFSPA.

Akal Takhat - Painting "Akal Boonga at the Golden Temple", 1864
William Simpson / V&A's collections

Tension mounted in the whole of Punjab as it prepared to commemorate the June 3 *Shaheedi Gurpurab*, the martyrdom day of Guru Arjan, the fifth spiritual master of the Sikhs. This was the time in Punjab when all the Gurdwaras, including the *Darbar Sahib* complex, would fill to capacity with thousands of devotees. Every village, home, and business would soon host *Chhabeels* – tent stalls – offering free rose-flavored chilled milk to thirsty passersby in the hottest month of summer.

This time around, the atmosphere was tense. Police and security forces pointed loaded guns at men, women, and children if they

Shaheedi: Martyrdom
Gurpurab: A day in commemorations of the Sikh Gurus

met in large groups or ventured outside their homes after hours, denying them the centuries-old tradition. Yet, since no formal curfew had been put into place, thousands traveled to visit Darbar Sahib, Amritsar, unaware of the danger to come – as they did every year, to pay respects to Guru Arjan who had built the edifice himself. Others came to participate in the *Akali Dal* agitation.

Little did they know that Amritsar was soon to be the setting for the third *ghallughara* – the genocide of the Sikhs.

Unsuspecting devotees trapped inside the Darbar Sahib Complex as security forces seal it before launching Operation Blue Star, June 1984 - Satpal Danish

Operation Blue Star

Jaswant was attending the *Panchayat* Secretaries' meeting in Patiala when he heard from his colleagues that the whole of Punjab was under lock down and had been cut off from outside without any warning. All communications, including phone lines to and from Punjab, were being cut. Roadblocks prevented anyone from entering or leaving Punjab, and all journalists were being expelled from the state.

On June 1, 1984, the Indian government launched "Operation Blue Star," a full-scale military assault on over forty Gurdwaras throughout Punjab. The primary assault concentrated on the *Darbar Sahib* and the *Akal Takhat* in Amritsar, an attack that had been planned many months in advance by the Indian Army.

According to an eye witness, Devinder Singh Duggal, a historian who had been in charge of the Sikh Reference Library of the *Darbar Sahib*, Amritsar, the army began firing into the complex from outside at about 12:30 p.m. on June 1, as *Sant* Bhindrawale sat on the roof of the Langar Hall. Army snipers opened fire on his group. Seven hours of gunfire left eight people dead. There were bullet holes in the Langar Hall, in the *parkarma*, the marble pavement surrounding the *Darbar Sahib* building. According to his account, there had been no gunfire from inside as *Sant* Bhindrawale had instructed the Sikhs not to retaliate unless the army entered the *Darbar Sahib* Complex.

Akal Takhat: Immortal Throne - the political seat of the Sikhs built by Guru Hargobind, the sixth Guru, in 1606, right across from the *Darbar Sahib*, the spiritual seat

However, on the evening news of the state-run All India Radio, it was reported that there had been an unprovoked attack on the army from inside the complex. Newscasts did not explain the killing of the eight people inside the complex or the more than thirty-six bullet holes in the *Darbar Sahib* building.

The day of June 2 passed peacefully, lending a semblance of a return to normalcy. People continued visiting the *Darbar Sahib*. The Sikhs killed on June 1 were taken to be cremated. In a national address, Prime Minister Indira Gandhi made a speech saying, "I appeal. Don't shed blood, shed hatred," knowing full well the extent of the blood her troops planned to shed in the following days.

On June 3, thousands of visitors entered the *Darbar Sahib* complex to commemorate the *Shaheedi Gurpurab*. They were mostly innocent villagers who had no idea of the state of affairs and had come with family and friends in their tractor-trailers or trucks to pay their respects to Guru Arjan. Hundreds of them were volunteers who had come to donate and serve in the *langar*, the community kitchen, as part of a tradition that feeds tens of thousands of visitors every day. There were also 1,300 *Akali* workers who had come to participate in the protest, the *Dharam Yudh Morcha*. There were no blockades preventing people from entering Amritsar and the *Darbar Sahib*. Visitors were given no warning of the attack and were allowed to enter freely.

Towards the end of the day, the Indian government forces sealed the exits to the *Darbar Sahib* Complex, trapping as many as ten-thousand visitors inside. They had no idea of the horror that would be unleashed upon them in the next three days and the scars that would haunt them for the rest of their lives if they managed to escape alive.

A handful of armed Sikh militants anticipated the government's intentions. They were ready to defend the complex and the devotees, and fight against the army's attack. Ex-Major General of the Indian Army, Shabeg Singh, a decorated war veteran who had played an important role in the victory of the 1971 war for the liberation of Bangladesh, led the plan to defend the *Darbar Sahib* in case of attack.

General Shabeg Singh and *Sant* Bhindrawale had advance knowledge of the Indian Army's sinister plan for the attack on the *Darbar Sahib.* As per their defense strategy, they fortified the *Akal Takhat* with sandbags and gun emplacements at the first sign of troops deploying in Punjab.

The day arrived when they would need to retain the honor of their tradition and resist tyranny with their lives. They would be no match for one of the largest armies in the world, but at least they would die as soldiers, as Guru Hargobind the master of *Miri* and *Piri* and the creator of the *Akal Takhat* had ordained.

On June 4, 1984, at around 4:00 a.m., the army started bombing and firing into the complex. The assault continued until the evening of June 6. Besides unleashing fierce machine-gun fire, the army troops also threw mortar shells and poisonous gas canisters inside the *Akal Takhat* and other buildings in the complex. Resistance from the armed fighters in the *Akal Takhat* lasted for several hours. Soldiers in helicopters fired and shelled from the air as well, killing many people and mutilating their bodies beyond recognition.

Miri and Piri: Sovereignty and Spirituality; Sikhs are instructed to be Saint-Soldiers; Devotion and Activism are both considered equally important aspects of Sikhi

Fires in the Darbar Sahib complex during Operation Blue Star

The army blasted the water tank and the top of the eighteenth-century towers called the *Ramgarhia Bungey*, setting ablaze many other buildings in the complex. The attack was so fierce and heavy that an artillery shell landed more than five kilometers away in another crowded area of Amritsar.

On June 5, late into the night, armored vehicles, including thirteen tanks moved into the complex, ramming into the *parkarma*, crushing its delicate marble inlays and shooting everyone on sight. The gunfire and shelling went on all night long. Exercising no restraint, the army fired directly at the *Darbar Sahib,* the *sanctum-sanctorum*, killing Amrik Singh, the blind and elderly *Head Raagi* who was attending the holy scripture, the *Guru Granth Sahib*.

Head *Raagi*: Lead hymn singer

In the early hours of June 6, the army increased the ferocity of their attack and started firing large cannon balls towards the *Akal Takhat,* killing anyone who came their way – men, women, or children. The entire front of the *Akal Takhat* was wrecked, and fires broke out in many locations, destroying the delicately embellished architecture and artwork dating back to the time of Maharaja Ranjit Singh. The defenders fought back bravely until the last man perished. The *Akal Takhat* was reduced to rubble after being subjected to repeated explosions.

Women and children who had barricaded themselves in rooms desperately ran out after poisonous gas shells started suffocating them. The army didn't hesitate to shoot even the women carrying babies.

Akal Takhat after the Operation Blue Star

Bodies of the devotees in the Darbar Sahib complex after Operation Blue Star

Soldiers prevented those still alive from leaving the complex, and many of the wounded were left to bleed to death or die of thirst. In the hot month of June, when temperatures consistently soared above forty degrees Celsius, those who used to serve *chhabeels* to chill others were forced to squeeze their shirts and drink sweat, for the vast *Amrit Sarovar* had turned red with the blood running from thousands of dead bodies all around it. No attempts were made to tend to the wounded; instead they were trampled by the army boots and left to die.

Hearing of the attack, nearly one hundred thousand Sikhs gathered in various villages and towns surrounding Amritsar including Mehta Chowk, Harike-Pattan and Batala to oppose the army action. They

Amrit Sarovar: Literally, the nectar pool - water pond surrounding the *Darbar Sahib* building

marched towards *Darbar Sahib* from different directions. They were met with fierce machine-gun fire from land and air, killing many.

Brahma Chellaney, an Associated Press (AP) correspondent, had managed to dodge the authorities and remain in the city during Operation Blue Star. He reported, "Amritsar was shaken by powerful shelling, mortar explosions and machine-gun fire. Tracer bullets and flares lit up the sky. The explosions at the Golden Temple rattled doors and windows miles away. While the battle was raging, the state-run radio claimed that the city was 'calm.' Between 10:30 PM and midnight, we heard slogans from city outskirts of villagers trying to march to the Golden Temple from three different directions. The slogans, 'Long live the Sikh faith' and 'Bhindrawale is our leader,' were heard on each occasion, and were followed by rapid army machine-gun fire and screams."

Later, Chellaney reported that dead bodies were taken in municipal garbage trucks round the clock and burnt in heaps of twenty or more. One attendant at the city's crematorium told him that there was not

Executors of Operation Blue Star: (left to right) Maj Gen K.S. Brar, Gen K. Sundarji and Gen A. S. Vaidya at Darbar Sahib after Operation Blue Star - India Today

"enough wood to burn the dead individually." Between June 7 and June 10, the Indian Army took control of the whole complex, searched every corner, drove any survivors out, and continued the killings. They also took into captivity 379 civilians whom they called the "most dangerous terrorists," and forced them to sign a common confessional statement declaring they were *Sant* Bhindrawale's close associates and were waging a war against the state. They were detained in Jodhpur Jail without trial for years and came to be known as the "Jodhpur detainees."

The Sikh Reference Library, with its priceless ancient manuscripts including some written by the Gurus themselves, documents, and historical artifacts, was burned and looted. Soldiers celebrated by drinking and smoking in the holy shrine, desecrating it without remorse, and hoisting the tricolor flag of India after taking down the *Nishan Sahib*, the Sikh flag.

While the Indian Army carried out a bloodbath in Amritsar, close to five thousand Sikh soldiers stationed elsewhere in Punjab, Rajasthan, Maharashtra, Gujarat, Bihar, West Bengal, and Uttar Pradesh marched towards Amritsar to protect the *Darbar Sahib*. Approximately eighty of them were killed by their own commanders or peers. Those who survived were imprisoned, dishonorably discharged from the army, and stripped of their privileges and pensions. The soldiers who participated in these mutinies later came to be known by the Sikhs as "*Dharmi Faujis*" or "Soldiers of the Faith."

Sant Bhindrawale, along with his two close associates, General Shabegh Singh and Bhai Amrik Singh embraced martyrdom defending the *Darbar Sahib*. Some 227 years earlier, in 1757, another Head of *Damdami Taksal*, Baba Deep Singh, too, had laid down his life, fighting Ahmad Shah Durrani, the invader

and desecrator of the *Darbar Sahib*. With his martyrdom, *Sant* Bhindrawale secured for all time a place of honor in the Sikh psyche.

The Indian government claimed that only 554 people had been killed and 121 injured in Operation Blue Star throughout Punjab. Given the attendance on the day of the attack, the eye-witness accounts, the photographs, the truckloads of bodies hauled away for mass cremation, and the number of unclaimed shoes at the shoe depository, the number of people killed at the *Darbar Sahib* Amritsar alone is conservatively estimated to be ten thousand.

The government claimed that the attack was meant to flush out militants and separatists in the *Darbar Sahib* Amritsar. They did not explain why its timing coincided with the *Shaheedi Gurpurab*. They also did not explain the attack on *forty-two** other Gurdwaras throughout Punjab, which inflicted heavy casualties as well.

Police had free access to the *Darbar Sahib* Complex just as anyone else would. Mark Tully, a BBC reporter, had interviewed *Sant* Bhindrawale just days before the attack. But no warrants were issued or attempts made to arrest anyone prior to the attack. The Deputy Commissioner of Amritsar, Gurdev Singh, had repeatedly and clearly informed the highest officials of the Punjab government that if they wanted to arrest *Sant* Bhindrawale, he would easily arrange it and had warned the Governor against using military force to do so. He was told there were no such plans.

In 1983, The Vice Chief of Army Staff (Western Army Command), Lieutenant General S.K. Sinha, refused to plan the attack at the *Darbar Sahib* as asked by Prime Minister Indira Gandhi. He was removed from the command of the Western Army and denied promotion

---

*The government white paper mentions action in forty-two other Gurdwaras, however the number is believed to be much greater

as the Chief of Army Staff. Reported army maneuvers on replicas of the *Darbar Sahib* complex in the Chakrata Hills also point to the intention and pre-planning of the government. It is widely believed that Operation Blue Star was executed to teach Sikhs a lesson and that the circumstances were created by the government itself.

Dr. Joyce Pettigrew, an Irish anthropologist who studied Sikhs and Punjab for more than forty years, summarized the operation well: "The army went into *Darbar Sahib* not to eliminate a political figure or a political movement but to suppress the culture of a people, to attack their heart, to strike a blow at their spirit and self-confidence."

Punjab was placed under military rule for the whole month. The Indian government cut off all communication, censored media reports and barred relief organizations from entering the state. Sikhs throughout the world went numb. Their faith in Indian democracy had been shaken forever. They felt wounded, helpless, and homeless once again.

Village Khalra, located along the border of India and Pakistan, was under special scrutiny as the Indian government suspected Pakistan's involvement in the armed struggle. It was believed that the border was used to smuggle and supply arms to the Sikh rebels in Punjab. Armed forces patrolled the village, harassing people. Jaswant's family worried about his safety as he was away in Patiala and there was no communication. Their eyes glued to the door, they prayed for him to come back. A week or so later, Jaswant made his way home with great difficulty. Together, his family mourned the assault on *Darbar Sahib*, the very essence of their being. Jaswant felt that life had been sucked out of him.

Together, the family cried, embracing each other, and as the tears settled down, they sat down to pray.

The Christian Science Monitor

June 8, 1984

"On Saturday, medical workers in Amritsar said soldiers had threatened to shoot them if they gave food or water to Sikh pilgrims wounded in the attack and lying in the hospital."

"For five days, the Punjab has been cut off from the rest of the world. There is a 24-hour curfew. All telephone and telex lines are cut. No foreigners are permitted entry and on Tuesday, all Indian journalists were expelled. There are no newspapers, no trains, no buses – not even a bullock cart can move. Orders to shoot on sight were widely carried out. The whole of Punjab, with its 5,000* villages and 50 major cities, was turned into a concentration camp. The rules were what the Indian Army and its political decision makers decided."

The Times

June 13, 1984

"The same doctor told journalists that bodies of victims were brought to the mortuary by police in municipal refuse lorries and reported that of the 400 bodies, 100 were women and between 15-20 were children under five. One was a two month old baby. The doctor said that one 'extremist' in the pile of bodies was found to be alive; a soldier shot and killed him."

---

* Actual number 12,278

THE SIKH MESSENGER

1984 - A resident of Amritsar's eyewitness account to the editor of the British Sikh publication

"On the night of the 5th, the aged and chronically ill father of the couple next door finally expired and on the morning of the 6th the army gave our neighbours special permission to take him to the crematorium. Even before reaching this site, they could smell the stench of putrid and burning flesh. On entering the crematorium grounds they saw a sight that literally made them sick with horror. Grotesque piles of dozens of bodies were being burnt in the open without dignity or religious rites like so many carcasses. The bodies had all been brought there by dust carts and from the number of carts; the attendant estimated some 3,300 had so far been cremated."

THE SUNDAY TIMES

June 22, 1984 - Mary Anne Weaver

"Thousands of people have disappeared from the Punjab since the siege of the Sikh's Golden Temple here weeks ago. In some villages men between 15-35 have been bound, blindfolded and taken away. Their fate is unknown. Recently in the tiny village of Kaimbwala, 300 troops entered the Sikh Temple during prayers, blindfolded the 30 worshippers and pushed them into the streets. According to the priest, *Sant* Pritpal Singh, the villagers were given electric shocks and interrogated as to the whereabouts of Sikh militants. Gurnam Singh, a 37 year old farmer was held in an army camp for 13 days. Last week, his face bruised and his arms and legs dotted with burns, he said he had been hung upside down and beaten."

November 1984
The Ghallughara Continues

It is said that the first casualty of war is truth.

As the Sikh community worldwide attempted to cope with the shock, distress, and details of the brutality emerging from eye-witness accounts from Operation Blue Star, the government was busy covering up the truth and propagating falsehood to justify the operation. It spread disinformation on the number and quality of the arms confiscated, fabricated criminal acts happening in the *Darbar Sahib* before Operation Blue Star, and exaggerated the threats from the *Dhararm Yudh Morcha*, labeling it a violent secessionist movement that conspired to create the state of Khalistan through terrorist activities.

The extent of the disinformation spread by the Indian government is evident from the June 10, 1984, Times of India front page headlines on a Press Trust of India report that read, "Terrorists made a desperate attempt to blow up the *Akal Takhat*, killed a number of men, women and children, and unsuccessfully tried to escape with huge amounts of cash, jewelry and other valuables after their leaders were killed in the action on June 5. The *Akal Takhat* was not damaged in the Army action."

Such disinformation and propaganda humiliated Sikhs worldwide as they were dealing with their grief.

The government also released a "White Paper* on Punjab Agitation" which grossly understated the extent of the destruction

White Paper: An authoritative report issued by the government

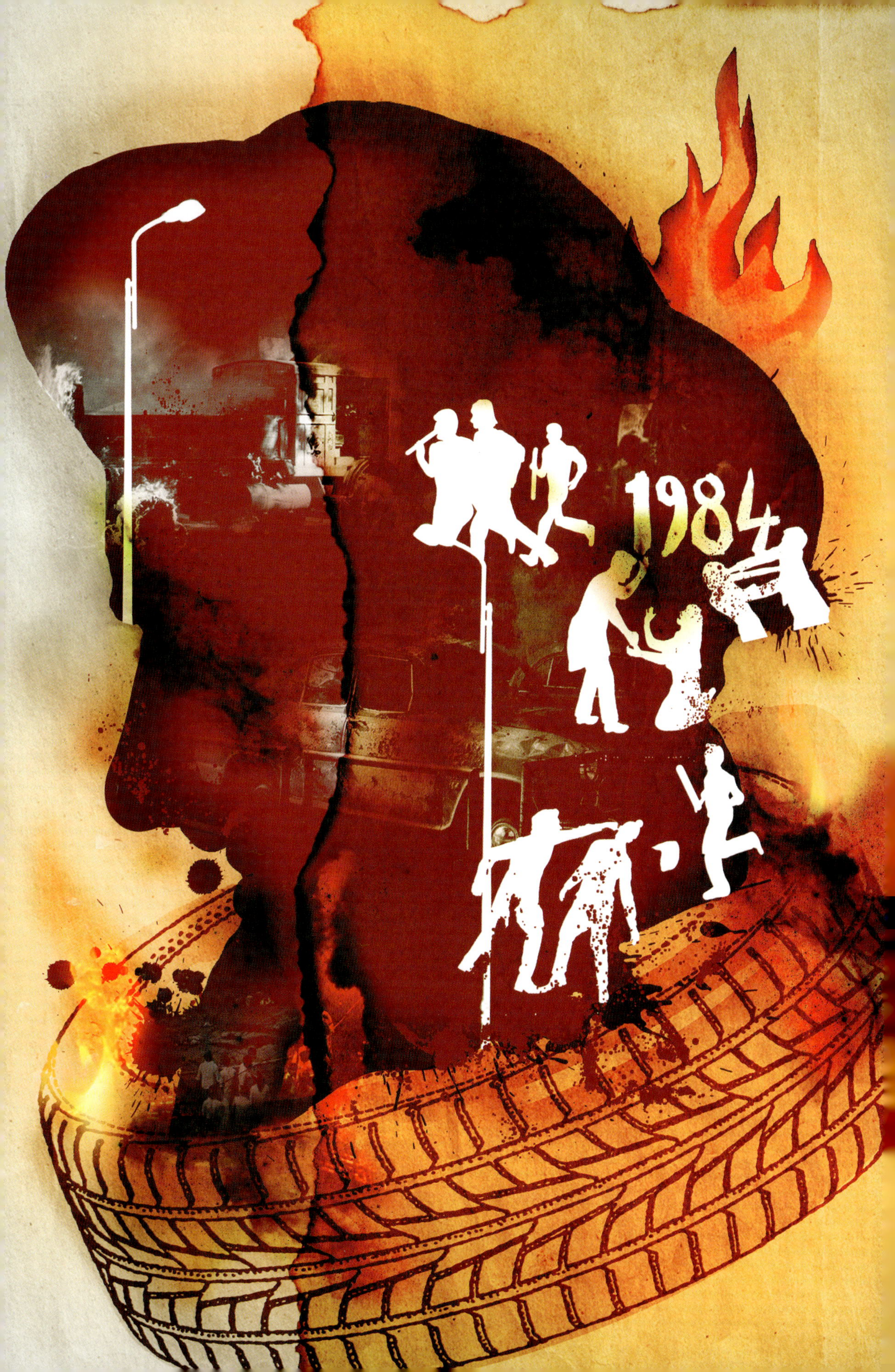
1984

and the killings. The Indian media obediently echoed all the lies the government was handing it, and spread them to the world. International media was already barred from Punjab so the extent of the operation and the truth on the ground did not receive the worldwide attention that such a violation of human rights should have garnered.

Anyone who dared to speak the truth was charged with sedition* and labeled anti-national. That included the Associated Press reporter, Brahma Chellaney, and the activists from Citizens for Democracy*, who interviewed several survivors and key witnesses to lay out the truth behind the operation in their report, "Oppression in Punjab." The investigative team was led by Justice V. M. Tarkunde, a prominent lawyer, civil rights activist, and a distinguished former judge of the Bombay High Court. A day after the publication of the report, it was banned and confiscated, and the authors were arrested and charged with sedition.

Thus, a large-scale massacre carried out by a government against its own citizens went largely unquestioned and unnoticed by human rights organizations around the world.

Their success in hiding this atrocity from the rest of the world emboldened the government of Prime Minister Indira Gandhi. She and her Congress party were now considered heroes on the Indian scene, having taken down the "enemy of the country, *Sant* Bhindrawale." Their prospects in the next elections looked good, really good – all at the expense of a minority that contributed more than any other community to India at every step, and in every field.

Sedition: Incitement of rebellion against a government

Citizens for Democracy: A reputed civil liberties organization in India founded in 1974

Despite being merely two percent of India's population, Sikhs led the struggle for the freedom of the subcontinent from the British *Raj*. Seventy-one percent of those who died in the struggle and eighty-one percent of those who were imprisoned for life by the British were Sikhs. Fifty-six percent of those who died fighting for the British Indian Army in the two world wars were Sikhs.

In 1947, approximately forty percent of the total Sikh population was forced to leave their homes and hundreds of places of religious and historical significance behind, and between five and eight percent of their total population perished during the partition of Punjab.

Sikhs formed the backbone of the Indian Army and made major contribution to the wars India fought with her neighbors. They contributed greatly to the Indian economy, too. Punjab was always known as the bread-basket of India. A dominant share of agricultural produce for India came from Punjabi Sikh farmers. And yet, once again, they were butchered for someone's political aspirations.

But, the bloodshed of June 1984 paled in comparison to what was yet to come in November 1984.

On October 31, 1984, the Indian news media reported that two Sikh members of Prime Minister Indira Gandhi's security staff, Satwant Singh and Beant Singh, had assassinated her in Delhi. According to the reports, they were acting in retaliation for the June massacre and the desecration of the *Darbar Sahib*, Amritsar. Reportedly, both were captured alive, however, Beant Singh was later killed.

The death of Indira Gandhi was broadcast all over the electronic and print media, sensationalizing the Sikh factor without any investigation, irresponsibly inciting retaliation towards the minority community. The same day, Mrs. Gandhi's son, Rajiv Gandhi, a newcomer to politics, took the oath as Prime Minister. Television and radio networks repeated broadcasts of his party supporters chanting, "Blood for blood" throughout the evening, inflaming the nation against the Sikhs – not just the alleged shooters, but all Sikhs nationwide. Senior politicians and police officers orchestrated systematic violence against Sikhs throughout the country with full government backing and a tacit assurance of impunity.

Soon after the assassination, the state machinery set itself in motion. After rousing the country's sympathy for the Gandhi family and setting the stage for revenge, they spread rumors that trains full of dead Hindus were arriving from Punjab, and that Sikhs had poisoned the Delhi water supply.

They organized, incited, and lured mobs in every major city, town, and village of India to unleash their hostility on Sikhs, and to teach them a lesson because they had killed the "Mother of the Nation." They equipped party workers with municipality records, voting lists, and paint, and they sent them out to mark Sikh homes and businesses.

In the three days that followed, from November 1 to November 3, 1984, the Congress Party organized, armed, and incited violent mobs to murder Sikhs and to loot and then set ablaze their homes, businesses, and places of worship. Neither Sikh schools nor hospitals were spared, even though they benefited non-Sikhs as well.

Mobs would pull Sikhs out of their homes, beat them, douse kerosene over them, and set them ablaze with burning tires around their necks while their helpless families were forced to watch. Their cries failed to move the hearts of even the ones who knew them well as their neighbors. The mobs were supplied with ample

KHOON KA
BADLA KHOON

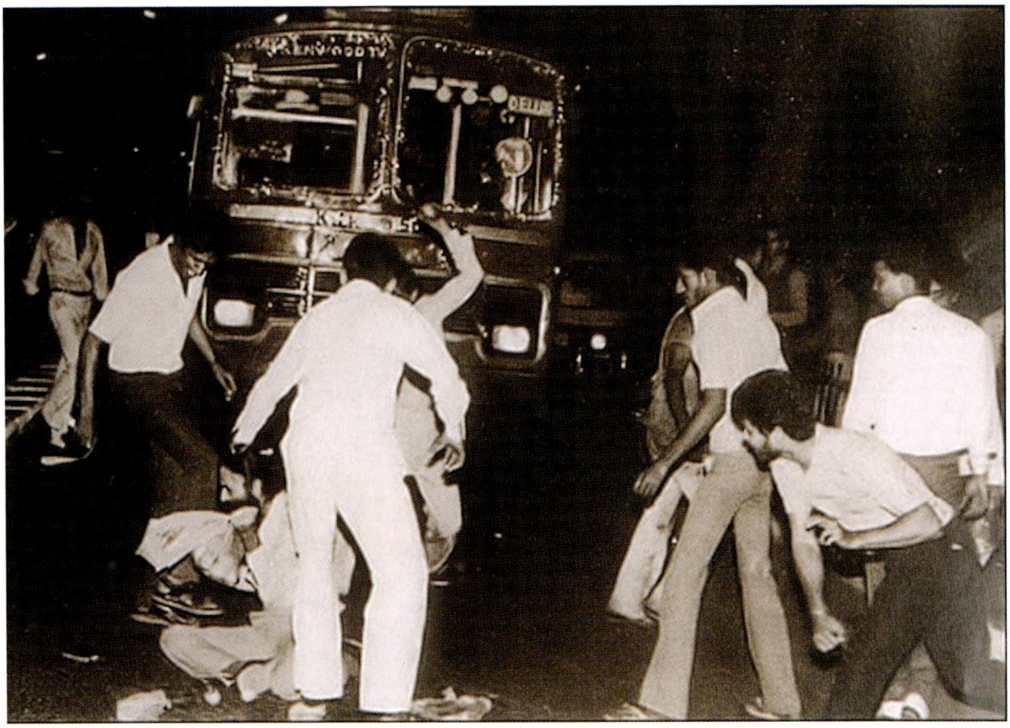

A mob in the act of lynching a Sikh truck driver in November 1984 pogroms

A mob setting alight four Sikh brothers and their paint shop, Delhi, November 1984

ammunition – iron rods, kerosene, tires, paint – and a list to check off. Hindu extremist groups in India, such as the *Shiv Sena* and the *Bajrang Dal*, readily joined hands with the Congress party workers and lent them their organizational know-how and manpower even though, historically, they had always been politically opposed to each other. The pogroms were executed in the same pattern everywhere in the country, indicating advance knowledge and a common plan.

Countless mothers and daughters saw the male members of their families, infants included, set on fire before their eyes.

Countless men saw their mothers, wives, daughters, and sisters gang-raped before they themselves were tortured and killed.

Countless men were scalped, or their hair was shorn to dishonor their faith even in their last moments, before they were set ablaze.

Sikhs traveling in automobiles, buses, and trains were seized and lynched by mobs waiting for them on the roads and at stations. Sikhs working in steel plants were dunked into hot boilers by their co-employees. Sikh truck drivers carrying goods throughout the country were stopped, pulled out of their cabs, and ruthlessly beaten to death, the goods looted, and their trucks set afire.

The police stood by and looked the other way, or even actively participated in the violence by inciting the mobs. Where the Sikhs were armed and ready to defend themselves, the police came and disarmed them before the mobs arrived. Government transportation such as the DTC, the Delhi Transport Corporation, carried mobs by the busload from one Sikh-inhabited area to another to carry out this rampage.

Some from other communities wanted to help and protect the Sikhs, but they were threatened by mobs or the police. With the exception of a few good Samaritans who risked their lives to help their innocent neighbors, the whole country watched silently, as though consenting to the treatment meted out to the Sikhs.

Through the media, the government spread rumors that provoked more violence against Sikhs for the next three days. When human rights activists, prudent journalists, and honest government functionaries started questioning the Ministers, they were only told that the government was working to bring the situation under control.

The Indian Army that had been so efficiently deployed in Punjab in the context of a handful of staged killings of Hindus, strangely, could not be deployed to stop the killing of thousands upon thousands of Sikhs throughout India until many days after the horrific massacres.

The Sikhs serving in the Delhi Police were locked up so they would not get in the way of the pogroms in the country's capital, where the majority of Sikhs outside of Punjab lived. Rajiv Gandhi, the new Prime Minister of India, when confronted by a journalist on his inaction to curb the violence, stated as justification, "When a big tree falls, the earth trembles a bit."

Not only did the government and police officials who led the pogroms do so with impunity, many were rewarded and promoted. Several years and seven commissions of inquiry later, no sentences were handed down. Arun Nehru, Kamal Nath, Sajjan Kumar, Jagdish Tytler, Dharam Das Shashtri, Bhajan Lal, HKL Bhagat, Arjun Das, and Lalit Maken – the men believed to be the chief orchestrators of the Delhi pogrom, all enjoyed high positions and promotions in the party or in the Indian government after their gruesome roles in the carnage.

In the government-sponsored pogrom, more than fifty thousand Sikhs were displaced and an estimated twenty thousand murdered in the capital city of New Delhi alone, the epicenter of the carnage. The total estimates for the whole of the country would be much greater. No investigation or inquiry into pogroms in cities other than New Delhi was ever undertaken.

Once again, the government lied about the magnitude of the killings. According to the official figure, 2,733 Sikhs were killed in the massacre in what the government labeled as "The Delhi Sikh Riots." The government did not even acknowledge the systematic murders of Sikhs that had taken place in hundreds of other cities, towns, and villages in India. A November 1984 incident that came to light twenty-seven years later in the year 2011 involved the brutal killing of all of the sixteen Sikh families of the village Hond Chillar in district Rewari of Haryana state. There may be many more of such hitherto unreported atrocities.

A site of mass murder in Hond Chillar (Rewari, Haryana) where all the Sikhs in the village were murdered and their homes burnt in the November 1984 pogroms

A mother looks fearfully in the aftermath of the violence, Delhi, November 1984

On November 15, 1984, Mary Anne Weaver, citing Rahul Bedi - a reporter from the Indian Express, reported in the Christian Science Monitor, that when Bedi arrived at Trilokpuri - a Sikh neighborhood of New Delhi, early Friday afternoon, to find the entrance sealed by police constables who said, "Nothing much was happening. It's all over. Maybe one or two people had been killed." However, when Bedi and another reporter made their way to Block 32; they found the road leading to the temple "carpeted with bodies, two or three deep, for a distance of nearly 50 feet." This was the scale of discrepancies between official accounts and the reality.

The pogroms were also labeled as "1984 Riots" by the government in its continued strategy to justify the action as a Hindu-Sikh communal rift resulting from the Hindu killings in Punjab. Yet, there were no Sikh groups or a single Sikh that came out on the roads, incited violence, or attacked a single Hindu following the June 1984 or November carnage, even in Punjab where the Sikhs were a majority.

Citizens for Democracy noted that "despite all the oppression of the Sikh community, there was no incident of a communal riot even in villages where the Hindus were in a hopeless minority."

Ghallughara is the Sikh term for a large-scale massacre, carnage, or genocide that happened as an act of persecution directed towards the Sikhs in their five-century-long history, a term which has become an integral part of the Sikh psyche.

In the year 1746, the first or the smaller *(Chhota) Ghallughara* took place when seven thousand Sikhs were killed in armed attack and three thousand were captured and later executed mercilessly in public in the streets of Lahore by the army of Lakhpat Rai and Yahya Khan. In 1762, the second or the larger *(Vadda) Ghallughara* took place when thirty-five thousand Sikhs were killed in Kup

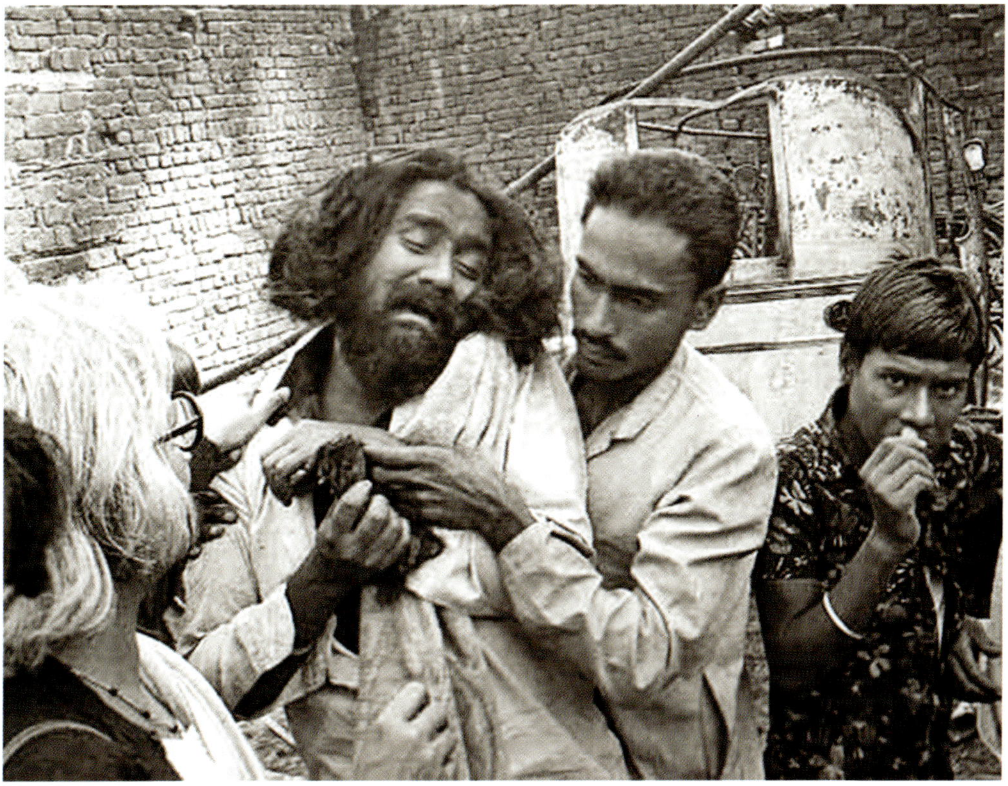

A survivor grieving at a refugee camp - Ram Rahman

Rohira, by Ahmad Shah Durrani, also known as Abdali. The 1984 genocidal act by the government of India came to be termed as the third *Ghallughara*, where the number of Sikhs killed rivaled the previous two *Ghallugharas*.

Yet, the nightmare was far from over.

The New York Times reported about the refugee camps in Delhi which still housed close to 25,000 Sikhs on Nov 7, 1984 – "Both Indian and foreign journalists have been forbidden to enter the refugee camps set up by the government, presumably since many of them contain miserable-looking widows, children and men who were forced to shave their beards and cut their hair to escape death. Such shaving is a violation of Sikh religious custom and ignominy to proud Sikhs."

The Widow Colony* in Tilak Vihar, Delhi, thus carved on the map of the capital of the "largest democracy in the world," is a living testimony to the horror faced by Sikh women in November 1984.

Most Sikhs felt too insecure, humiliated, and devastated to go back to their homes. Many had lost all family members and everything they owned. Thousands of children were orphaned.

The state government of Punjab opened its doors for the rehabilitation of the Sikhs displaced from Delhi and elsewhere in India who had lost everything, including the will to stay back.

Jaswant spent the following months helping rehabilitate the victims and working with press reporters to document their plight so that the stories of the carnage would never be forgotten.

Widow Colony: A settlement, west of New Delhi, housing widows of the Sikh men who were killed in the 1984 massacre

TIME

It's Time India Accept Responsibility for Its 1984 Sikh Genocide

October 31, 2014

Frenzied mobs of young Hindu thugs, thirsting for revenge, burned Sikh-owned stores to the ground, dragged Sikhs out of their homes, cars and trains, then clubbed them to death or set them aflame before raging off in search of other victims.

Witnesses watched with horror as the mobs walked the streets of New Delhi, gang-raping Sikh women, murdering Sikh men and burning down Sikh homes, businesses and Gurdwaras. Eyewitness accounts describe how law enforcement and government officials participated in the massacres by engaging in the violence, inciting civilians to seek vengeance and providing the mobs with weapons.

The pogroms continued unabated, and according to official reports, within three days nearly 3,000 Sikhs had been murdered, at a rate of one per minute at the peak of the violence. Unofficial death estimates are far higher, and human rights activists have identified specific individuals complicit in organizing and perpetrating the massacres.

"Almost as many Sikhs died in a few days in India in 1984 than all the deaths and disappearances in Chile during the 17-year military rule of Gen. Augusto Pinochet between 1973 and 1990," pointed out Barbara Crossette, a former New York Times bureau chief in New Delhi, in a report for World Policy Journal.

Thirty years later, those who survived the violence have yet to receive any semblance of justice. Most perpetrators have yet to be charged and held accountable for their crimes, and many of the affected families continue to live in poverty and disenfranchisement to this day. The Indian government's formal position for three decades has been that accountability comes in the form of silence.

The Indian government is certainly not the first to massacre its own citizenry. Yet, as Crossette points out, so many of the nations complicit in ethnic cleansing – including Chile, Argentina, Rwanda and South Africa-have recognized the importance of addressing past atrocities. Yet the Indian state stubbornly refuses to admit its fault and take ownership of its participation in mass violence, despite enormous evidence to the contrary.

THE
WIRE

Fighting Fatalism, 35 Years After the Anti-Sikh Pogroms

November 1, 2019

"Certain images had to be burned into the psyche," reported journalist Ivan Fera. "How else to explain the fact that the men were not merely killed but tortured to death – limb severed from limb, eyes gouged out, burnt while they were still alive – in instance after instance, all over the city, in the very presence of their children and their wives? The killings were ritualistic: in several cases the hair of the victim were shorn off, and their beards set on fire before they were killed."

Sikh women were ferociously targeted, often in front of their families, including through individual and gang rape, in some cases lasting over multiple days.

MANUSHI

Forum for Women's Rights and and Democratic Reforms

Gangster Rule: Massacre of the Sikhs in 1984

1985

Madhu Kishwar, editor of Manushi, writes: "Many eyewitnesses confirm that the attackers were not so much a frenzied mob as a set of men who had a task to perform and went about it in an unhurried manner, as if certain that they need not fear intervention by the police or anyone else. When their initial attacks were repulsed, they retired temporarily but returned again and again in waves until they had done exactly what they meant to do – killed the men and boys, raped women, looted property and burnt houses."

ਅੰਧਿਆਰੇ ਦੀਪਕੁ ਚਹੀਐ॥

In the darkness, we need a lamp.

Bhagat Kabeer, SGGS: 655

THE CALLING

Move to Amritsar

The distraught couple, Jaswant and Paramjit, lived in village Khalra for a few more months following the events of 1984. In 1985, four years after they married, they were blessed with a little girl whom they named Navkiran, meaning, "a new ray of light."

Soon after Navkiran's birth, Paramjit began her dream job as an assistant librarian at the Bhai Gurdas Library of Guru Nanak Dev University. The family moved to Amritsar, some 40 kilometers from Khalra, so she could pursue her career. Jaswant still kept his job in the village and commuted between Khalra and Amritsar.

On July 25, 1985, Rajiv Gandhi negotiated the so-called "Peace Accord" with the then *Akali Dal* leader, Harcharan Singh Longowal. The accord promised to transfer Chandigarh to Punjab, to set tribunals to sort out river water and territorial disputes, to heed to the center-state framework in favor of state autonomy, to begin inquiries into the November 1984 pogroms, to withdraw the draconian Armed Forces Special Powers Act, and to restore human rights in Punjab, among other demands from the Anandpur Sahib Resolution. However, twenty-six days after Harcharan Singh Longowal signed the accord, he was assassinated by militants who called the signing of a treaty with the government that desecrated the *Darbar Sahib* an act of betrayal.

Surjit Singh Barnala, the succeeding *Akali* leader, who had also mediated the Peace Accord, led the *Akali Dal* to a victory in the state assembly elections that followed in September 1985. It was hoped that this victory would usher Punjab into an era of peace based on the Peace Accord.

BHAI GURDAS LIBRARY
ਦਮਨ ਵਿਰੋਧੀ ਫਰੰਟ
FRONT AGAINST OPPRESSION
ਗੁਰ ਗਿਆਨ ਦੀਪਕ ਉਜਿਆਰੀਆ
THE LAMP OF GURU'S WISDOM SHINES FORTH.

However, on January 26, 1986, when Chandigarh was to be transferred to Punjab, newspapers reported the government's decision to backtrack. The government did not honor any part of the accord. This led to an escalation in militancy. Counter-insurgency operations by the government also increased. The situation in Punjab continued to deteriorate.

Jaswant became alarmed over reports from newspapers portraying Sikhs as terrorists engaged in armed rebellion, as robbers and murderers of innocent Hindus.

The government-controlled media published pictures of police officers posing alongside the dead bodies of Sikhs and their purported weaponry. They claimed those Sikhs had been terrorists, killed in so called "encounters" with the police force.

Yet, when Jaswant went to the villages to speak to the families of the deceased, he found that they had been picked up by the police on the pretext of interrogation just a day or two before the news reports came. To hide the evidence of their crimes, security forces secretly disposed of the bodies, either by cremating them or by dumping them in water canals. This happened so frequently that Jaswant devoted the majority of his time to looking into the cases of custodial torture, disappearances, and killings in fake encounters, dropping all other priorities. He formed an organization called *Daman Virodhi* Front, or "Front against Oppression." This was a group of like-minded activists who raised their voices against arbitrary detentions, custodial torture, disappearances, and fake encounters by the police, and at the same time, any excesses by the militants. They also let the world know what was actually going on in Punjab.

Security forces in Punjab posing next to Sikhs killed in a staged encounter

The Khalistan Movement

As the government attempted to crush the *Dharam Yudh Morcha* to appease and win favor with the Indian majority community, its atrocities caused more and more Sikh youth to take up arms and engage in armed rebellion against the government.

Fueled by Operation Blue Star, the India-wide pogroms of November 1984, and the central government's repudiation of the 1985 Peace Accord, the armed insurgency in Punjab saw a boost. To handle the insurgency, the central government brought in an officer named K.P.S. Gill, who was transferred to Punjab from the state of Assam where he had served as the "Police In-Charge."*

K.P.S. Gill was a ruthless man who vowed to put down any rebellion in Punjab by brute force. He used his powers indiscriminately. A dark period of disappearances and fake encounters involving Sikh youth throughout rural Punjab had begun, all in the name of the counterinsurgency.

In 1986, K.P.S. Gill was promoted to the position of Inspector General.

In the meanwhile, frustrated by the insincerity and the evasiveness of the government in fulfilling any of the provisions of the Peace Accord, the Sikh groups called for a *Sarbat Khalsa* to discuss the collective will and path for the community.

Police In-Charge: Chief police officer of the state

Sarbat Khalsa is a convening of the entire Sikh commonwealth, whereby representative bodies of the *panth* gather at the *Akal Takhat* when the *panth* is facing a critical issue that necessitates a collective will to resolve. Leaders from the Sikh bodies meet in the presence of the *Guru Granth Sahib* and discuss matters of policy and action regarding the issue at hand. The deliberation begins with an *Ardaas*, and the decisions are made with common counsel in an environment where personal animosities are put aside, and patriotism, unity, and the good of the *panth* are the driving forces. When the *Gurmatta* is passed, the prayers are again said with its declaration. The first recorded *Sarbat Khalsa* dates back to 1726.

At the *Sarbat Khalsa* held at the *Akal Takhat* on January 26, 1986, the gathering passed a *Gurmatta* asking the Sikhs to break the shackles of slavery and injustice from India. Another gathering held there on April 29, 1986, declared the creation of Khalistan, a sovereign Sikh nation-state.

The government escalated its operations even further while gaining worldwide sympathy based on the possible dismemberment of India by the Khalistan movement.

On April 30, 1986, the very next day after the declaration of Khalistan, the government launched Operation "Black Thunder - I." Approximately 300 National Security Guards commandos along with 700 Border Security Force troops stormed the *Darbar Sahib* and captured about 200 Sikhs, killing and injuring several. There was no provocation or armed resistance by the Sikhs.

Ardaas: Community prayer
Panth: Community, nation
Gurmatta: Resolution by Sarbat Khalsa

Sarbat Khalsa at Akal Takhat, Amritsar, January 26, 1986

In December 1986, the Central Reserve Police Force (CRPF), a para military force of the Indian Army, opened fire in a Gurdwara and killed several innocent Sikhs in the village of Bramhpura in Tarn Taran district very close to Amritsar in a frustrated attempt to capture a militant leader, Avtar Singh Brahma.

In protest of such indiscriminate violence by the state, Jaswant began an indefinite hunger strike in front of the city police office in Tarn Taran, precipitating his arrest for the second time in his life. This was only a few months after Paramjit Kaur had given birth to their second child, Janmeet Singh.

On May 11, 1987, the central government dismissed the *Akali* Punjab government and imposed President's Rule, taking Punjab under its direct governance. India's Parliament enacted further legislation that freed security forces from any accountability for violating human rights under the guise of national security.

"The Terrorist and Disruptive Activities (Prevention) Act (TADA)," enacted in 1985 specifically to deal with the insurgency in Punjab, was amended in 1987 to provide the police with the powers of search, seizure, and arrest of anyone they suspected might be a threat to India. Police routinely used torture to obtain confessions from detainees and / or planted evidence as a means of detaining them under TADA, whereupon the defendants themselves had the burden of proving their innocence.

In 1988, K.P.S. Gill, who was now the Director General of the Punjab Police (DGP), launched Operation "Black Thunder - II" in the *Darbar Sahib*, Amritsar under the pretext of rooting out the militants taking cover there, killing several and arresting hundreds. It had become the norm for security forces to enter any Gurdwara without notice and terrorize the faithful.

Jaswant, who had recently been released from his previous arrest, could not tolerate this act of the government and organized a large demonstration to protest it. He aimed to bring such atrocities to the attention of the media and the world. He was arrested once again and imprisoned in the city of Ludhiana.

While Jaswant continued his activism, helping people, looking after his village responsibilities and courting arrest, Paramjit was raising two infants, managing a job, and running the family primarily on her own. It was her contributions that allowed Jaswant to dedicate so much of his time and energy to the cause.

Upon his release from jail, Jaswant came across case after case where young men had been picked up by the security agencies on the pretext of interrogation, never to be heard from again. Often the families had to bribe the police to retrieve the bodies of the loved ones who had been tortured and killed.

Violence from the state was met by violence from militants who targeted cruel police officers and sectarian leaders in retaliation. Both sides escalated their attacks, resulting in the loss of innumerable lives. Under the cover of militancy, criminals began to coerce businessmen and landowners, demanding protection money. Some attempted to settle personal vendettas by posing as militants. The government trained special agents known as "Black Cats" with the purpose of infiltrating the militant groups in order to discredit them. Disguised as militants, they committed atrocities against common people. Infighting ensued within the militant groups, now infiltrated by government agents and unsure of who was on which side. The movement that began as a noble struggle for human rights came under the grip of intelligence agencies, and degenerated to a communal and vengeance-driven movement that trampled on human rights.

Jaswant despaired at the mindless violence on both sides. While he was against the government atrocities, he also openly criticized the militants for targeting innocent civilians. He went on a five-day hunger strike to protest the killing of Hindus by "unidentified armed militants" in his area, despite being warned against condemning the militant groups. Jaswant maintained that if the taking of innocent lives by the state was wrong, it was equally wrong for the militants. He said that unless the revolution had the discipline to strictly enforce the safeguarding of innocent lives, its cause would cease to be legitimate.

The Threat Mounts

In November 1987, to address the human rights violations and as an act of protest against the government, Jaswant Singh formally resigned from his position as the *Panchayat* Secretary of his village.

Like his fellow volunteers at the *Daman Virodhi* Front, he now devoted all his time to investigating the cases of people under imminent threat of torture and elimination following their illegal detention. The cases poured in faster than they could count.

In a few cases, Jaswant and his team procured the release of those who had been illegally detained by proving their innocence. Even though such cases were rare and there was a danger to his own life in fighting against the all-powerful state, saving even one life gave Jaswant immense satisfaction and the conviction to continue on this path.

In 1989, the political situation in the central government changed with the defeat of Rajiv Gandhi and his party. The new government promised restoration of peace in Punjab through negotiations. However, nothing changed, and violence perpetrated by both the state and the state-infiltrated militant groups continued to distress Punjab.

The implication of police officers later revealed the hand of the police in some killings that were attributed to militant groups in order to portray those groups as dangerous. Then police officers would kill a member of that militant outfit to get rewards and promotions.

As Jaswant continued to help the victims of such atrocities and to highlight their occurrences, threats to his life became more rampant.

Under tremendous pressure from family and friends to safeguard his life, Jaswant Singh flew to England in 1990 and applied for political asylum, which was granted to him.

Jaswant Singh with Paramjit Kaur and their children at his brother's wedding, 1989 - Family collection

Jaswant Singh holding his daughter Navkiran and son Janmeet, 1987 - Family collection

Jaswant Singh with his Mother Mukhtiar Kaur, 1989 - Family collection

The Darkest Hour

In November 1991, Punjab was brought under the Disturbed Areas Act, a law which gave the security forces even more power to search, detain, and interrogate anyone without a judicial warrant. Under these conditions, in January 1992, elections were held in Punjab and boycotted by the *Akali Dal* and its supporters who wanted to first see these inhumane laws repealed. The boycott was called for and enforced by Sikh militant groups. They held the view that without other elements of democracy – human rights, freedom of expression, freedom of faith – the elections were a sham.

With *Akali Dal*'s boycott of the elections, and less than twenty percent voter turnout, the Congress party was declared the winner in the state. Beant Singh was installed as the Chief Minister of Punjab against the will of the majority. His assignment was to keep the world from finding out that Punjab was simmering and to bring a semblance of normalcy to the state. The news of human rights abuses in Punjab was starting to embarrass the Indian government internationally, and they felt the need to quietly restore law and order in Punjab.

Instead, the Beant Singh regime ushered in the worst human rights abuses Punjab had ever seen. The government eliminated anyone who embarrassed it or got in the way of establishing a false semblance of normalcy. They silenced the reporters and human rights activists who publicized state torture, disappearances, and fake encounters.

Punjab Human Rights Organization (PHRO) was next on their list. PHRO, a human rights organization founded in 1985, investigated

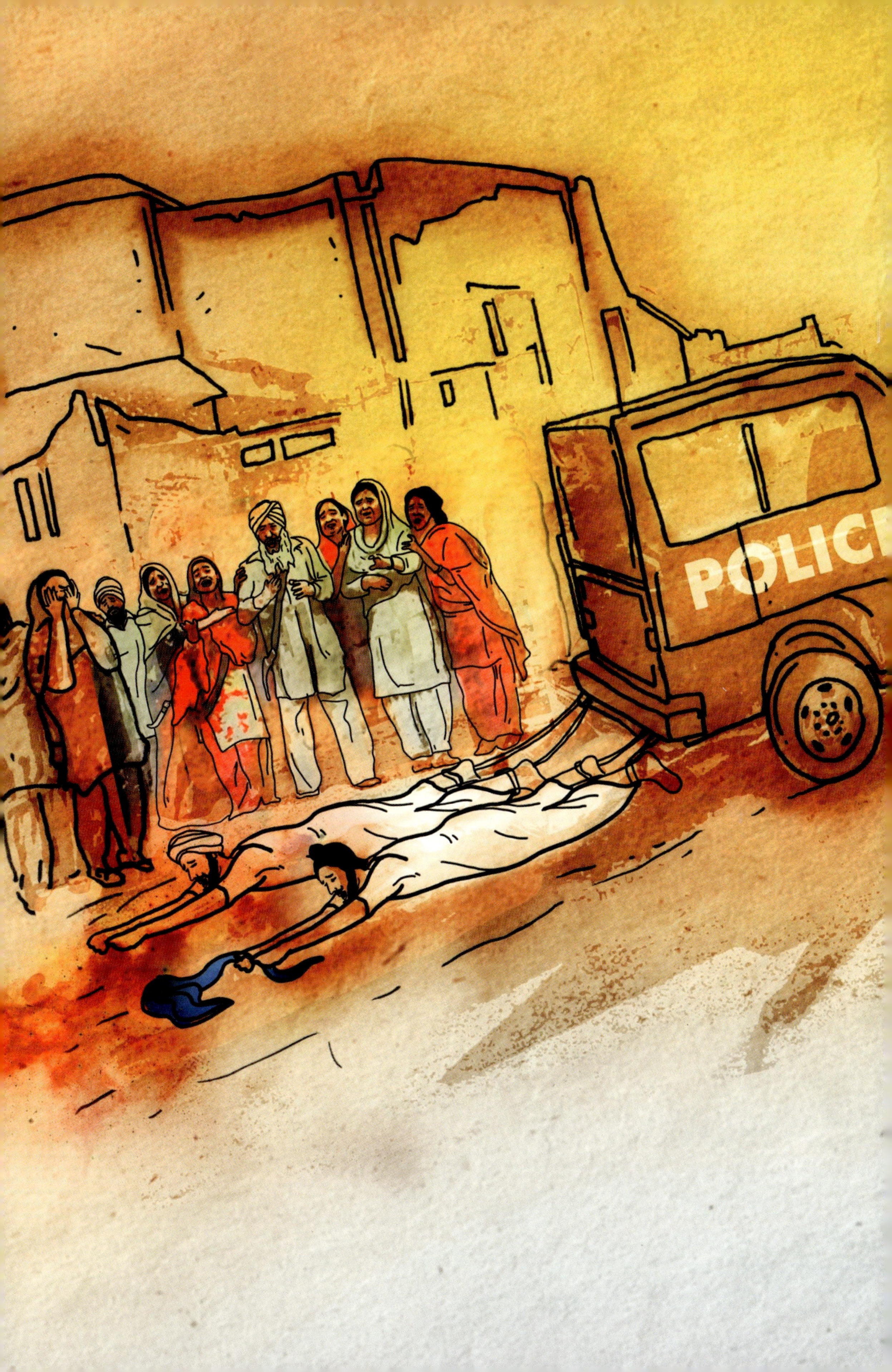
POLICE

cases of human rights violations, including disappearances, kidnappings, extrajudicial executions, and beatings and torture in detention. The police arrested Ajit Singh Bains, a retired High Court judge, the chairman of PHRO, who defended the arrested civilians in the courts, and Malwinder Singh Malli, the General Secretary, who published several reports on police torture. Ram Singh Biling, the Secretary of the PHRO and Jagwinder Singh, a human rights lawyer who fought to free innocent civilians, were detained and then murdered by the police to intimidate other such activists.

Many student activists from various universities who were associated with the PHRO or other human rights organizations and who spoke out against government atrocities were also arrested, tortured, or disappeared.

K.P.S. Gill introduced a system of incentives for policemen who killed militants, encouraging them to resort to extrajudicial executions and disappearances. The central government created a special fund to

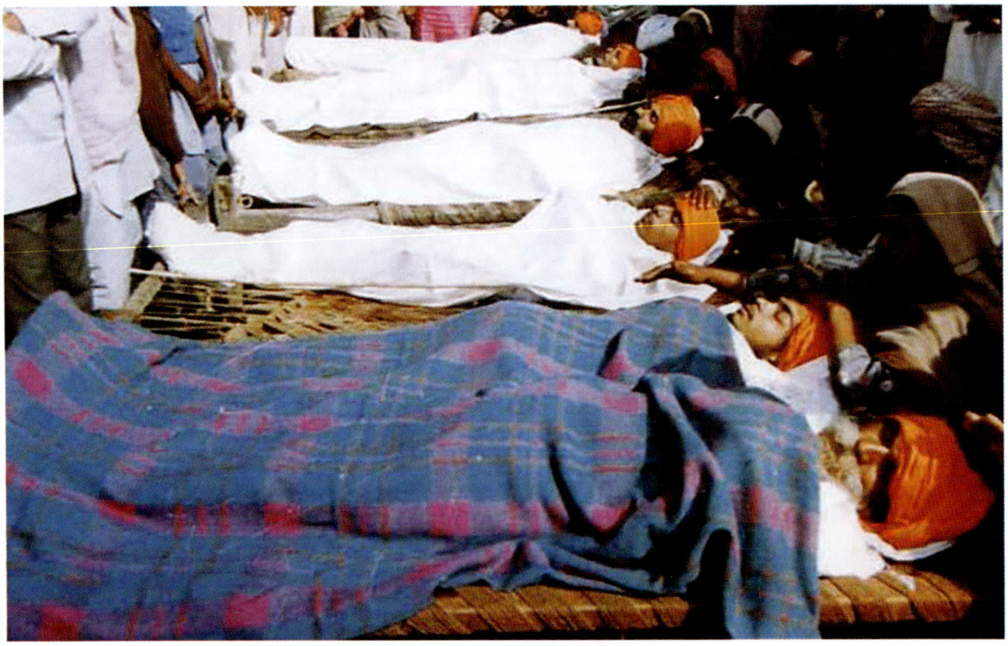

Bodies of members of a family killed in a staged police encounter

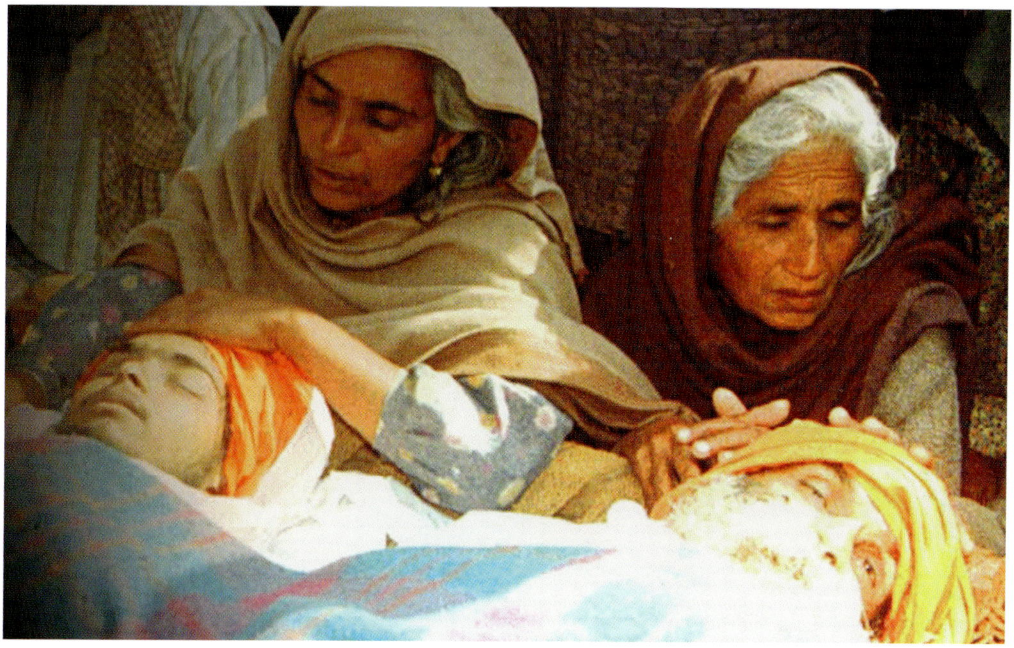

finance these executions and to reward the informants in return for information on suspected militants and their sympathizers. On October 15, 1992, the news magazine, India Today, reported that "the rush of claiming cash rewards is turning police into mercenaries." At the same time, K.P.S. Gill did not hesitate to punish the honest policemen who refused to be a part of the state executions. They met with the same fate as the suspected militants.

Within six months of assuming office, the Beant Singh government with K.P.S. Gill as its Police In-Charge, claimed to have curbed the Sikh militant movement. Several groups were either eliminated or forced to surrender. Then the government focused on cleansing the villages of sympathizers and the families of the militants. They spared neither women nor children.

Inhumane treatment, including mutilation, cruelty, and torture of prisoners is specifically prohibited by the Universal Declaration of Human Rights, as proclaimed by the United Nations General

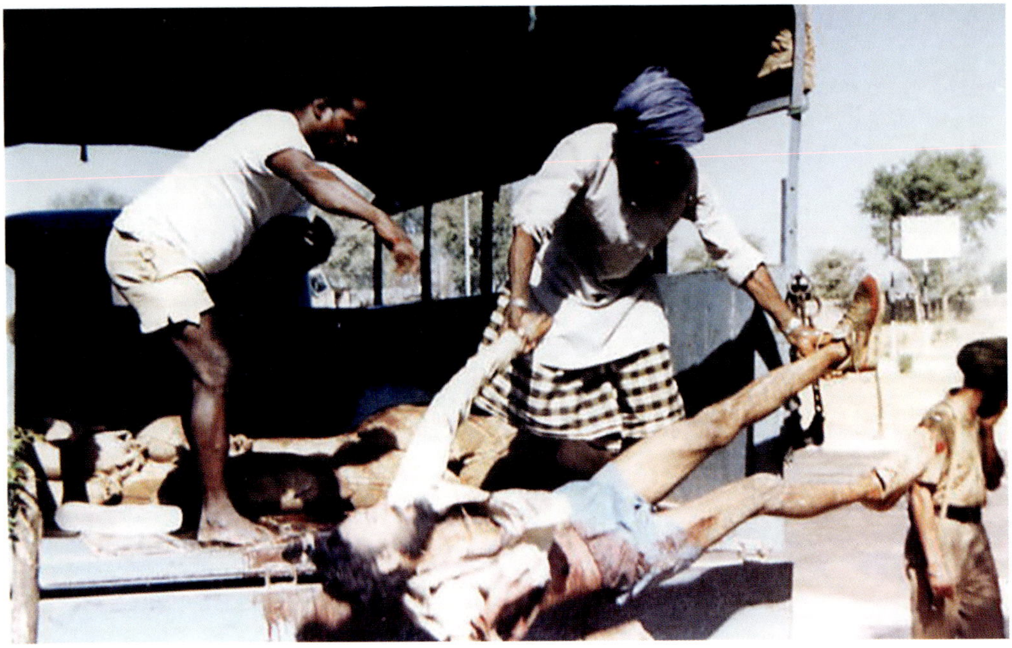

Sanitary workers loading the bodies of young Sikh men killed by the security forces

Assembly in Paris on December 10, 1948. India, being a member of the United Nations, is thus a party to the declaration.

In violation of this declaration, the security forces used extreme torture to interrogate the suspects and intimidate their families into giving information about the suspected militants. The security forces blackmailed the militants into surrender by torturing women, children, and elderly relatives in their families. Young girls and elderly mothers were not spared from rape or torture. Village upon village was emptied of *Amritdhari* Sikh men.

Thousands were tortured in police custody and brutally killed. Most families never received the bodies of their loved ones because the police either denied having detained them or said that the bodies were too disfigured to be identified. In rare cases where the bodies were returned, the police intimidated the families and supervised the cremations so that no pictures could be taken. Intimidation and

Amritdhari: Sikhs initiated into the Khalsa order

extortion of the frightened villagers became the norm.To whom could they go for help? Even the lowest ranking police employees threatened to arrest male members of any family if a ransom was not paid.

According to government figures, the security forces in Punjab killed 2,119 militants in the year 1992 under the term "encounters." However, the numbers again lie. Reports published in the Pioneer, an English daily published from New Delhi, suggested that many of the "disappeared" were killed and their bodies quietly dumped into Punjab's irrigation canals. These reports said that the government of Rajasthan, a neighboring state that receives downstream canal waters from Punjab, had formally complained to the Punjab Chief Secretary that the canals were carrying large number of dead bodies into the state.

These bodies, with their hands and feet tied together, were being fished out when water in-flow in canals was stopped for maintenance and repair work.

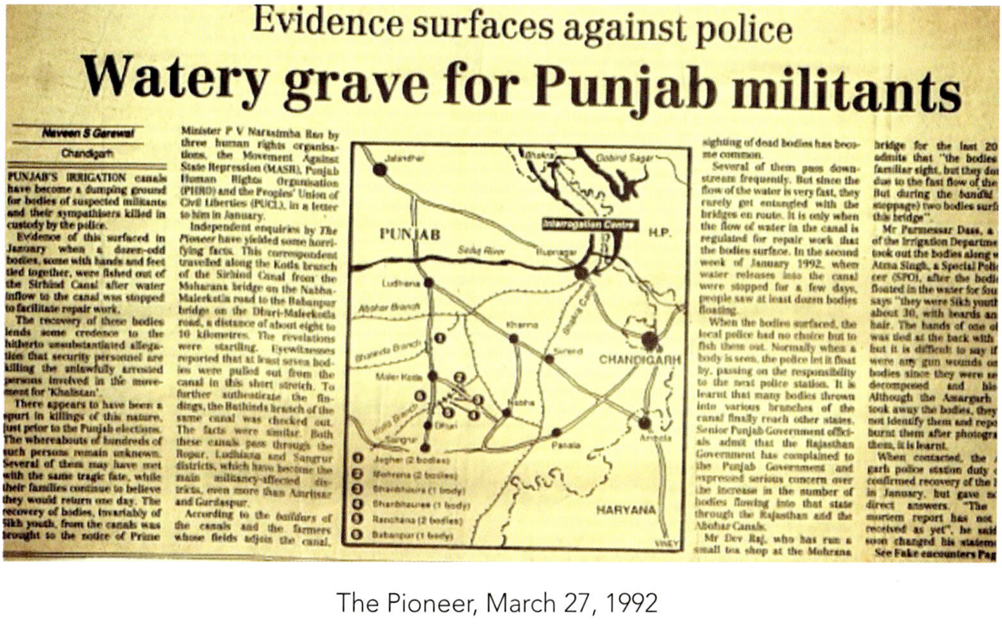

Evidence surfaces against police

Watery grave for Punjab militants

Naveen S Garewal
Chandigarh

PUNJAB'S IRRIGATION canals have become a dumping ground for bodies of suspected militants and their sympathisers killed in custody by the police.

Evidence of this surfaced in January when a dozen-odd bodies, some with hands and feet tied together, were fished out of the Sirhind Canal after water inflow to the canal was stopped to facilitate repair work.

The recovery of these bodies lends some credence to the hitherto unsubstantiated allegations that security personnel are killing the unlawfully arrested persons involved in the movement for 'Khalistan'.

There appears to have been a spurt in killings of this nature, just prior to the Punjab elections. The whereabouts of hundreds of such persons remain unknown. Several of them may have met with the same tragic fate, while their families continue to believe they would return one day. The recovery of bodies, invariably of Sikh youth, from the canals was brought to the notice of Prime Minister P V Narasimha Rao by three human rights organisations, the Movement Against State Repression (MASR), Punjab Human Rights Organisation (PHRO) and the Peoples' Union of Civil Liberties (PUCL), in a letter to him in January.

Independent enquiries by *The Pioneer* have yielded some horrifying facts. This correspondent travelled along the Kotla branch of the Sirhind Canal from the Maharana bridge on the Nabha-Malerkotla road to the Babanpur bridge on the Dhuri-Malerkotla road, a distance of about eight to 10 kilometres. The revelations were startling. Eyewitnesses reported that at least seven bodies were pulled out from the canal in this short stretch. To further authenticate the findings, the Bathinda branch of the same canal was checked out. The facts were similar. Both these canals pass through the Ropar, Ludhiana and Sangrur districts, which have become the main militancy-affected districts, even more than Amritsar and Gurdaspur.

According to the *beldars* of the canals and the farmers whose fields adjoin the canal, sighting of dead bodies has become common.

Several of them pass downstream frequently. But since the flow of the water is very fast, they rarely get entangled with the bridges en route. It is only when the flow of water in the canal is regulated for repair work that the bodies surface. In the second week of January 1992, when water releases into the canal were stopped for a few days, people saw at least dozen bodies floating.

When the bodies surfaced, the local police had no choice but to fish them out. Normally when a body is seen, the police let it float by, passing on the responsibility to the next police station. It is learnt that many bodies thrown into various branches of the canal finally reach other states. Senior Punjab Government officials admit that the Rajasthan Government has complained to the Punjab Government and expressed serious concern over the increase in the number of bodies flowing into that state through the Rajasthan and the Abohar Canals.

Mr Dev Raj, who has run a small tea shop at the Mohrana bridge for the last 20 ... admits that "the bodies ... familiar sight, but they d... due to the fast flow of the ... But during the *bandhi* ... stoppage) two bodies surf... this bridge".

Mr Parmessar Dass, a ... of the Irrigation Departme... took out the bodies along ... Atma Singh, a Special Poli... cer (SPO), after the bodi... floated in the water for fou... says "they were Sikh youth... about 30, with beards an... hair. The hands of one of ... was tied at the back with ... but it is difficult to say if ... were any gun wounds on ... bodies since they were ... decomposed and his... Although the Amargarh ... took away the bodies, they ... not identify them and repo... burnt them after photogra... them, it is learnt.

When contacted, the ... garh police station duty ... confirmed recovery of the ... in January, but gave no ... direct answers. "The ... mortem report has not ... received as yet", he said ... soon changed his stateme...

See Fake encounters Pag...

The Pioneer, March 27, 1992

ਬਿਨੁ ਤੇਲ ਦੀਵਾ ਕਿਉ ਜਲੈ॥੧॥ਰਹਾਉ॥

Without the oil, how can the lamp be lit?

Guru Baba Nanak, SGGS: 25

ROAD TO DESTINY

Punjab Calls

For two years, as Jaswant worked to establish a safer life in England, he was tormented by news of escalating atrocities in Punjab. He tried to continue in his role as a human rights activist from afar by speaking out about what was going on in Punjab and by seeking international attention. But he felt restless and helpless being unable to safeguard the lives of his fellow human beings. He withered in pain hearing about new cases every day.

When the rest of the family was preparing to join him in England, he stopped them, and, one day in 1992, without informing anyone, he showed up at his home in Amritsar when state terrorism was at its peak – to confront it with more determination than ever.

Jaswant was received with shock and fear for his life, but he tried to make his family feel comfortable. They failed to understand his motives. But Jaswant had risen above the love of self and family and had developed more clarity for his life's purpose than ever before.

Jaswant was determined to help families whose children had a chance of coming back if he did something about it. He wanted to stop these atrocities at all costs, and the only way in his mind was to relentlessly expose the government. Given what the government had done to the PHRO and other human rights activists, he knew that he had to be efficient and effective in a short period of time. He remembered what *Bapu-ji* used to say: if he wished to effect change, he must join a political establishment.

So Jaswant joined the Human Rights Wing of the *Akali Dal* as its General Secretary. He, along with other like-minded human rights activists, joined hands to make the *Akali Dal* adopt issues of law and justice as its main political agenda. They swiftly got to work helping the families of the disappeared to find their loved ones.

Jaswant Singh (first on left) at a protest in front of the Indian consulate, London, 1990 - Family collection

Jaswant Singh (second from left) with his brothers and parents, Khalra, 1994 - Family collection

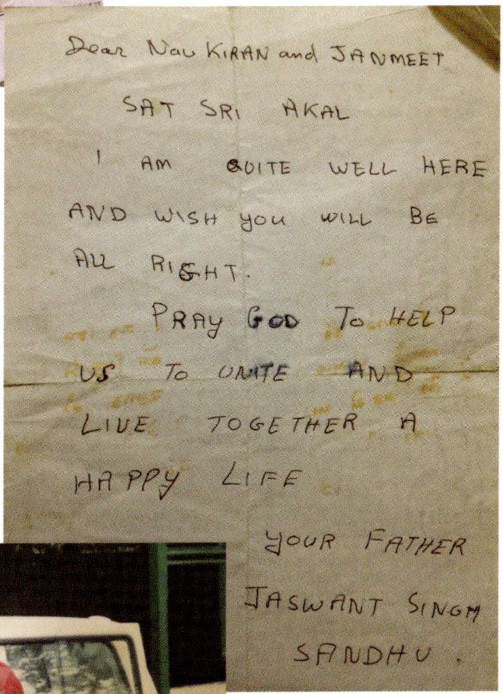

Dear Nav KIRAN and JANMEET

SAT SRI AKAL

I AM QUITE WELL HERE AND WISH YOU WILL BE ALL RIGHT.

PRAY GOD TO HELP US TO UNITE AND LIVE TOGETHER A HAPPY LIFE

YOUR FATHER
JASWANT SINGH
SANDHU.

Letter written by Jaswant Singh to his children from London, 1992 - Family collection

Paramjit Kaur with Navkiran and Janmeet at summer vacation, 1992 - Jaswant Singh / Family collection

A Sikh of Guru Nanak

Jaswant's upbringing as Guru Nanak's Sikh had taught him to stand up against injustice to anyone and everyone. He did not limit his stance to Punjab or to the Sikhs; he lent his voice to whomever he could help.

On December 6, 1992, a large group of Hindu activists from various sectarian organizations, led by the *Bhartiya Janata Party* (BJP), demolished the sixteenth-century Babri Mosque in the city of Ayodhya, situated in the North Indian state of U.P., chanting anti-Muslim slogans. This was all done against court orders, in the presence of the police. Ayodhya is believed to be the birthplace of the Hindu deity, Lord Rama. Some Hindus claimed that the site where the Babri Mosque stood was the exact site of Lord Rama's birthplace. However, the people opposed to this theory stated that such claims only arose in the eighteenth century, and that there was no evidence for the site being the birthplace of Lord Rama.

The destruction of the Babri Mosque sparked Muslim outrage around the country. Several months of inter-communal rioting followed in which Hindus and Muslims attacked one another, burning and looting homes, shops, and places of worship. Close to two thousand people died in the violence, most of them Muslims.

Jaswant was devastated and saw this as another offensive from the state on another of its minorities, the Muslims. Despite his

Bhartiya Janata Party: A Hindu nationalist political party in India

heavy involvement in Punjab, he decided to stand up against the oppression of a community that was wounded, vulnerable, and alone. He believed that as a Sikh, it was his duty to stand with the oppressed, especially when no one else would. He organized and participated in a hunger protest against the Government of India to raise awareness for the issue. His actions spoke clearly and conveyed the message that Indian Muslims were not alone in this dark hour of oppression.

Jaswant had hoped that the *Akali Dal*, which was founded on the Sikh principle of justice for all, would do the same. But Jaswant saw that the *Akali Dal* had joined hands with the BJP despite the BJP's open and radical stance against Muslims. After protesting and communicating his stance to the party, he detached himself from the *Akali Dal* in 1993.

He continued further investigations into human rights violations in Punjab, both independently and with his previous teams.

Babri Mosque, Ayodhya, before its demolition in 1992

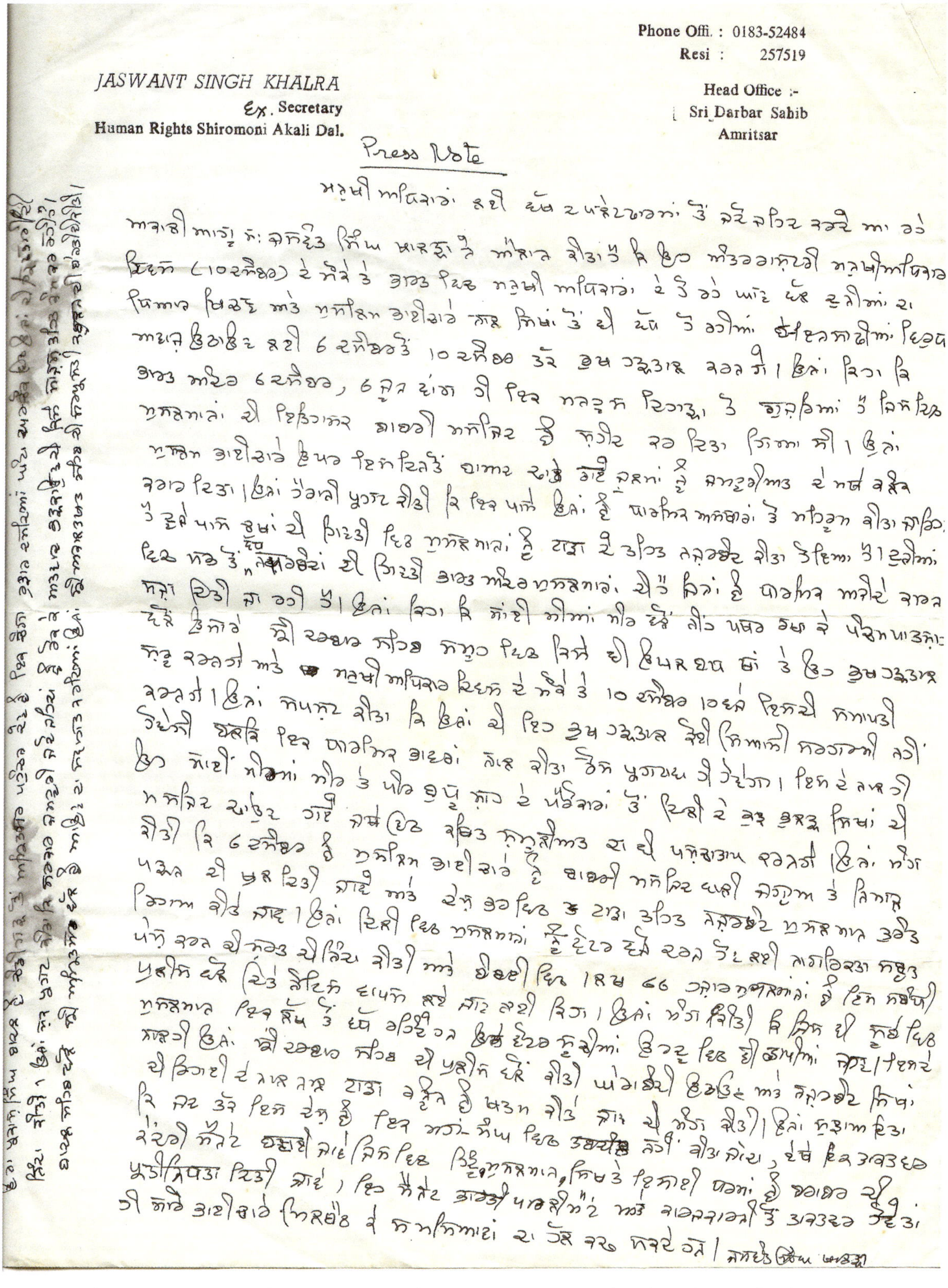

Handwritten press note by Jaswant Singh to protest against the demolition of Babri Mosque

The Key to Disappearances

For almost two years now, Jaswant was running from one village to another, trying to help families whose members had been picked up by the police. It was all about timing. If he and his team were approached in time, they could sometimes locate the kidnapped, and if they were lucky, they would be able to get the person released from police custody through the involvement of lawyers, locals, and family members before it was too late. However, those who had already been disappeared were at the complete mercy of their captors.

By now, the disappeared also included two of his colleagues.

On July 23, 1992, Piara Singh, the Director of the Central Cooperative Bank in Amritsar where Jaswant worked, was picked up from a relative's farm in Pilibhit, Uttar Pradesh, that he was visiting at the time.

On January 1, 1993, 28-year old Amrik Singh, another colleague of Jaswant's from the same bank was abducted from his home in village Mattewal, district Amritsar.

Jaswant had not anticipated that police brutality would come so close to him. He and his team desperately set out to look for his colleagues, but they found no leads. Around the same time, he heard about the abduction and disappearance of Mahinder Kaur of village Panjwar (presently in Tarn Taran district). She was the mother of a militant, Paramjit Singh, and had been picked up along with other relatives, both men and women, from the village. Jaswant

ਪੁਲਿਸ ਸਟੇਸਨ

was distraught that the security forces were now abducting and harassing female family members of suspected militants, too.

On February 27, 1993, newspapers reported that the police had shot dead a sought-after militant leader, Gurbachan Singh Manochahal, in an encounter. Many members of his family and village had been previously picked up by the police for interrogation; five of them, including his mother Gurmej Kaur, had disappeared, never to be seen again.

Jaswant had heard that Gurbachan Singh Manochahal's family was denied his body for cremation. Jaswant's organization *Daman Virodhi Front*, and the *Damdami Taksal* both publicly demanded that the body be handed to his family for cremation. When they inquired at the police station, they were told that Gurbachan Singh had already been cremated. With due investigation, Jaswant found that the body had been cremated at Tarn Taran crematorium and declared as a *lawaris*. He challenged the government as to why the body had been cremated as *lawaris* when there were many organizations asking for it.

That was also the key that led Jaswant and his team to the crematorium grounds in the area and opened the door to solving thousands upon thousands of disappearances, including those of his coworkers, Piara Singh and Amrik Singh. At the Durgiana Temple crematorium in Amritsar, Jaswant located the records of Piara Singh and Amrik Singh's cremations. They, too, were labeled *lawaris*. There, Jaswant also saw several unattended pyres. He decided to investigate cremations by the police by checking crematoria records.

Lawaris: Heirless, unclaimed

Puran Kaur
Shahbazpur Chhina, 1984

Amarjit Kaur
Amritsar, 1984

Jasbeer Kaur
Veroke, 1986

Surjit Kaur
Wahid, 1989

Gurmej Kaur
Lit, 1990

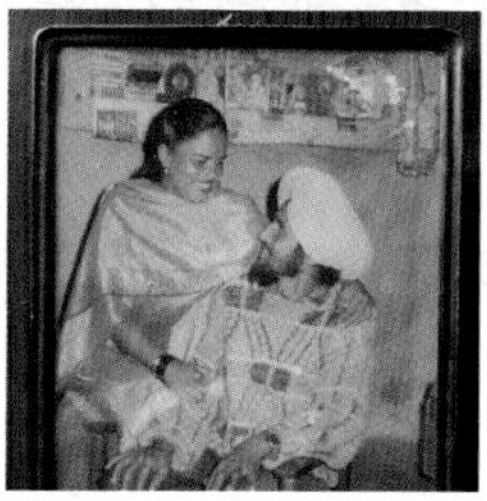

Gurwinder Kaur
Nathupur, 1990

Shinder Kaur
Kheri Musalmani, 1991

Manjit Kaur
Killi Bodla, 1991

Jaswinder Kaur
Killi Bodla, 1991

Surinder Kaur
Sagra, 1992

Kulbir Kaur
Raipur Kalan, 1992

Harbhajan Kaur
Tur, 1992

Joginder Kaur
Panjwar, 1992

Sawinder Kaur
Jaura, 1992

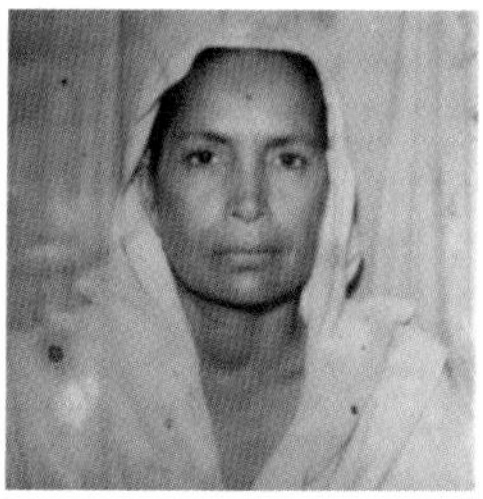

Hans Kaur
Mananwala, 1993

Sakina Begam
Bhama Kalan, 1993

Sukhwinder Kaur
Naushehra Pannuan, 1993

Jagir Kaur
Khojkipur, 1993

Gurmej Kaur
Naushehra Pannuan, 1993

Nasib Kaur
Rasulpur, 1992

Some women murdered by the security forces in Punjab - Ennsaaf

The Breakthrough

Until now, Jaswant and his team were following up on the large number of dead bodies showing up in the irrigation canals carrying water from Punjab into Rajasthan, but they were not getting anywhere as the bodies rotted in the water and were unidentifiable. It was also hard to figure out from where in Punjab were they being put into the canals.

After the crematorium lead, Jaswant and his team launched a full-scale investigation focusing on illegal cremations, putting aside other possible means of disposal of the victims' bodies for the time being.

Jaswant Singh and his co-activists, Amrik Singh Muktsar and Jaspal Singh Dhillon, went from one cremation ground to another looking for records. They asked employees about the number of dead bodies turned over to them by the police. Some reported burning eight to ten bodies daily. Others said that there was no way to keep an account; sometimes two to four dead bodies came and sometimes a truckload of them.

After much interrogation, a crematorium employee quietly confided in Jaswant: it was possible to get an accurate count in one place. The police brought them the dead bodies, and the municipal committee provided them with the firewood. But the firewood was only issued per dead body after all the records about the deceased were entered in the registers. The registers would be the source of evidence that Jaswant sought. They contained all the details of the deceased and the names of the police officers who had brought them there.

Jaswant's team went to investigate the crematoria in the cities of Amritsar, Patti, and Tarn Taran.

Patti is where the team had another breakthrough in their investigation. They pleaded with the crematorium employees to share their records on issuing the firewood used for pyres. The records were concealed, forbidden to be shared with anyone. Yet, all Jaswant and his team needed was one person, one person who would show them the registers, one person who valued truth and justice over the fear of losing his job, one person who felt strongly that the state was engaged in a killing spree and that someone needed to act.

At the Patti crematorium, the team found this one person, an elderly gentleman, and convinced him to share the information. He met the duo in secret and shared one of the register logs, whereupon Jaswant borrowed the records and made photocopies. The logs had all the details: the names of the deceased, their fathers' names, their villages, the police officer who brought them, and one last column that read, "*lawaris.*" In Patti, they found records for 538 such bodies cremated from January 1991 to October 1994.

"How could a deceased person's record contain so many details and yet still have his body declared *lawaris*?" questioned Jaswant.

The law said that if the police came across a dead body, they were required to locate the next of kin and notify them of the death. The law said that every deceased person had to be given his or her last rites with dignity. But in these cases, citizens had been denied not only their right to live, but also their due dignity and legal rights in death.

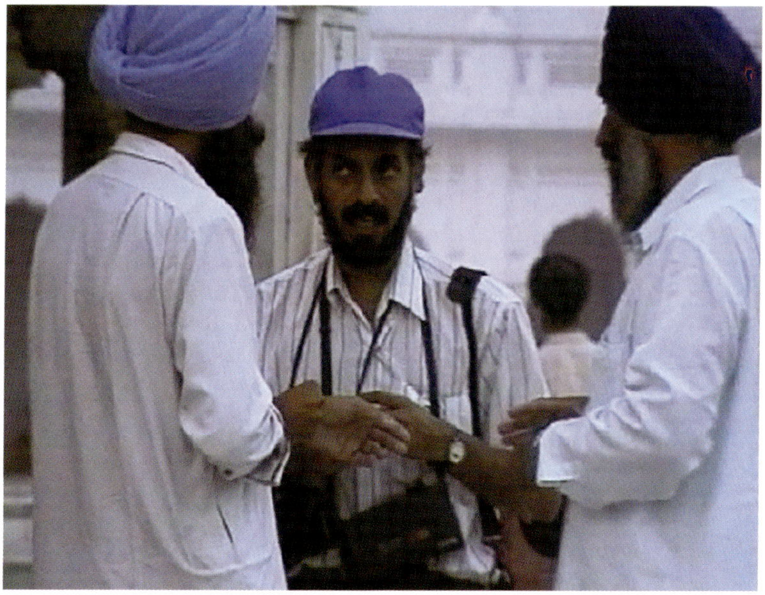

(Left to right) Jaspal Singh Dhillon, Ram Narayan Kumar and Jaswant Singh Khalra during field work for documenting the disappearances in Punjab, 1994 - Ram Narayan Kumar collection

1321	07-11-92	ਤਰਲੋਕ ਸਿੰਘ s/o ਜਰਨੈਲ ਸਿੰਘ ਵਾਸੀ ਤਹਿਸੀਲ ਪੱਟੀ	ਥਾਣਾ ਪੱਟੀ FIR 67/92 ਰਾਹੀ ਰਜਿਸਟਰ ਕੀਤਾ	ਲਾਵਾਰਿਸ
1322	01-02-93	ਗੁਰਦੀਪ ਸਿੰਘ s/o ਅਜੀਤ ਸਿੰਘ, ਵਾਸੀ ਕੈਰੋਂ	ਥਾਣਾ ਪੱਟੀ FIR 5/93 ਰਾਹੀ ਰਜਿਸਟਰ ਕੀਤਾ	ਲਾਵਾਰਿਸ
1323	6-2-93	ਸੁਖਦੇਵ ਸਿੰਘ ਉਰਫ ਲੱਖਾ s/o ਬਲਵੰਤ ਸਿੰਘ, ਵਾਸੀ ਬਾਹਮਣੀਵਾਲਾ	ਥਾਣਾ ਪੱਟੀ FIR 9/93 ਦੇ ਰਜਿਸਟਰ ਕੀਤਾ	ਲਾਵਾਰਿਸ
1324	6 6-2-93	ਬਲਦੇਵ ਸਿੰਘ ਉਰਫ ਗੁਰਦੇਵ ਸਿੰਘ s/o ਗਿਆਨ ਸਿੰਘ, ਵਾਸੀ ਗੁਰਦਾਸਪੁਰ	ਥਾਣਾ ਪੱਟੀ FIR 9/93 ਦੇ ਰਜਿਸਟਰ ਕੀਤਾ	ਲਾਵਾਰਿਸ
1325	18-2-93	ਮੁਖਤਿਆਰ ਸਿੰਘ ਉਰਫ ਮੁੱਖਾ s/o ਗੁਰਮੇਲ ਸਿੰਘ, ਵਾਸੀ ਲੋਹਕਾ	ਥਾਣਾ ਪੱਟੀ FIR 12/93 ਰਾਹੀ ਰਜਿਸਟਰ ਕੀਤਾ	ਲਾਵਾਰਿਸ
1326	18-4-93	ਪਰਗਟ ਸਿੰਘ ਉਰਫ ਪੱਗਾ s/o ਮੱਘਰ ਸਿੰਘ ਜੱਟ, ਵਾਸੀ ਸਰਹਾਲੀ ਮੰਡਾਂ	ਥਾਣਾ ਪੱਟੀ FIR 27/93 ਦੇ ਰਜਿਸਟਰ ਕੀਤਾ	ਲਾਵਾਰਿਸ
1327	18-4-93	ਬਖਸ਼ੀਸ਼ ਸਿੰਘ ਉਰਫ ਬੀਸ਼ਾ s/o ਤੇਗਾ ਸਿੰਘ ਮਜ਼੍ਹਬੀ, ਵਾਸੀ ਸੇਰੋਂ	ਥਾਣਾ ਪੱਟੀ FIR 27/93 ਰਾਹੀ ਰਜਿਸਟਰ ਕੀਤਾ	ਲਾਵਾਰਿਸ
1328	28-4-93	ਰੇਸ਼ਮ ਸਿੰਘ s/o ਸਾਧਾ ਸਿੰਘ ਜੱਟ, ਵਾਸੀ ਦੁਬਲੀ	ਥਾਣਾ ਪੱਟੀ FIR 28/93 ਰਾਹੀ ਰਜਿਸਟਰ ਕੀਤਾ	ਲਾਵਾਰਿਸ
1329	28-4-93	ਸੁਖਦੇਵ ਸਿੰਘ s/o ਜਗੀਰ ਸਿੰਘ ਵਾਸੀ ਤੈਰਾਨ	ਥਾਣਾ ਪੱਟੀ FIR 28/93 ਦੇ ਰਜਿਸਟਰ ਕੀਤਾ	ਲਾਵਾਰਿਸ
1330	28-4-93	ਕੁਲਵਿੰਦਰ ਸਿੰਘ ਉਰਫ ਸੁਖਵਿੰਦਰ ਸਿੰਘ s/o ਜੀਤ ਸਿੰਘ, ਵਾਸੀ ਜੌੜਾ	ਥਾਣਾ ਪੱਟੀ FIR 28/93 ਦੇ ਰਜਿਸਟਰ ਕੀਤਾ	ਲਾਵਾਰਿਸ
1331	14-6-93	ਪਰਮਜੀਤ ਸਿੰਘ ਉਰਫ ਪੰਮਾ s/o ਨਰਿੰਦਰ ਸਿੰਘ, ਵਾਸੀ ਬਾਹਮਣੀਵਾਲਾ	ਥਾਣਾ ਪੱਟੀ FIR 33/93 ਦੇ ਰਜਿਸਟਰ ਕੀਤਾ	ਲਾਵਾਰਿਸ

Recreated list of actual unlawful cremations from the NHRC public notice, July 19, 2004

While going through the records at Durgiana Mandir Amritsar crematorium, Jaswant found that in 1992 alone, the police had cremated 300 bodies designated as *lawaris*. This was in just one crematorium, in one city, in one year. There were hundreds of crematoria in Punjab. The mere thought of the potential magnitude of the disappearances shook Jaswant.

Jaswant had finally found the proof. A list of hundreds of dead bodies lay before him. What the team had known for years was now written in black and white, legal evidence of state-sponsored wrongdoing. They immediately made lists containing the names of the dead brought by specific police officers cremated at Durgiana Mandir, Tarn Taran, and Patti crematoria over several years and correlated them with the news on disappearances.

After gathering all the details, they went to the families listed in the records so they could urge the families to file reports and pursue legal action. Jaswant found that most families failed to believe that their loved ones were no more, and they still hoped to see them return some day. He could not convince many to report the disappearances because they were afraid of confronting the state. They believed that if their loved ones were still alive, the state would kill them in retaliation. Some felt that there was no hope for justice. They believed that if the state was the one that took the lives, then how could it mete out any justice?

There were many families in which every male member had disappeared. In others, both parents had been taken, and there were only the children or the elderly who remained. Despite these hurdles, Jaswant convinced some families to report disappearances and to begin to fight for justice; only to see them harassed by the police in the process.

Jaswant soon realized that the courts, too, refused to see, hear, or speak up when it came to human rights. At the same time, when the intelligence agencies discovered what Jaswant was gearing up to do, they became wary. They didn't want the world to know the truth about the human right abuses in Punjab. Jaswant began receiving death threats from the state security forces.

He needed to act quickly.

Jawant Singh (Second from right) and Jaspal Singh (right) talking to the family members of the disappeared, 1994 - Ram Narayan Kumar collection

An Act of Unparalleled Courage

On January 16, 1995, Jaswant Singh, Jaspal Singh, and their companions at the *Daman Virodhi* Front called a joint press conference in Chandigarh with the *Akali Dal* Human Rights Wing officials. Along with documented evidence, they released a press statement alleging that the police and the security forces in Punjab had engaged in the illegal abduction and murder of innocent people. They revealed that despite being aware of the identities of the deceased, the crematoria had secretly cremated them after labelling their bodies as *lawaris*. They stated that the law had been broken at every step, and they enumerated which laws and articles of the constitution were being brazenly violated.

The press statement detailed their investigations based on the firewood issuance logs revealing approximately 3,100 names (about 400 in Patti, 700 at Tarn Taran and 2000 in Durgiana Mandir) of disappeared persons in three crematoria in Amritsar district alone, Amritsar being just one of the thirteen districts of Punjab. Based on their investigations, research, and projections, they showed estimates leading to a total of 25,000 missing persons murdered by the state and illegally cremated in all thirteen districts over the previous ten years.

They provided several examples of well-known cases of state-sponsored abductions where the abductees ended up in a crematorium. They revealed the devastating stories of many families in Amritsar district who were unsure of what had happened to their loved ones, and who, in the absence of confirmation of death, were still waiting for closure. They could neither perform

(16) THE TRIBUNE, THURSDAY, JANUARY 19, 1995
'Missing persons' not killed: Gill
From Our Correspondent
AMRITSAR, Jan 18 – The government is seized with the problem of thousands of Sikh youth, who had gone to foreign countries under fake names and documents, and were claimed as "missing persons killed by security forces in encounters," the Director-General of the Punjab police, Mr K.P.S. Gill, said here today.
Talking to newspersons, he said there was a lot of confusion as the police had made lists of the missing persons. In most of the cases, the reports were not true as the persons were missing with the consent of their parents and relatives.
by changing their names and addresses, he added.
Referring to the situation in the state, Mr Gill said the ISI of Pakistan was doing its best to revive militancy in Punjab.
He said certain Sikh "Jathebandis", staying in foreign countries, were raising funds for the militants. There had been reports that a lot of money was being collected outside for granting "Pensions" to the militant families, however, a major chunk of this money
Skeletons in Punjab police cupboard
by S. P. S. Pannu
PATTI (Amritsar) – Damning evidence has surfaced of the bodies of suspected terrorists killed in police custody having been cremated as "unclaimed". This was done not only at the height of terrorism in Punjab but even after the situation had changed for the better.
Evidence gathered by Indian Express reveals that during the three-year period between 1991 and 1993 the Punjab police dumped at least
ists, still nurture hope of their returning home. While some families have moved habeas corpus petitions in the high court, several others have not done so for fear of police reprisals. Sources within the police disclosed that
PLEA REJECTED:

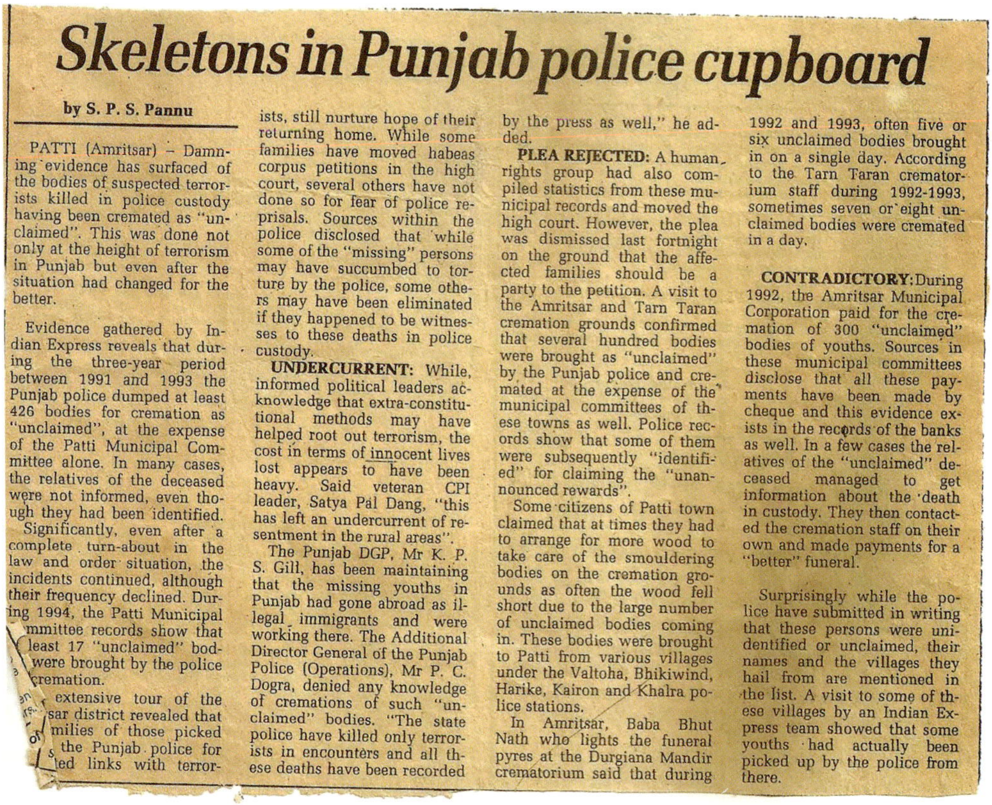

Skeletons in Punjab police cupboard

by S. P. S. Pannu

PATTI (Amritsar) – Damning evidence has surfaced of the bodies of suspected terrorists killed in police custody having been cremated as "unclaimed". This was done not only at the height of terrorism in Punjab but even after the situation had changed for the better.

Evidence gathered by Indian Express reveals that during the three-year period between 1991 and 1993 the Punjab police dumped at least 426 bodies for cremation as "unclaimed", at the expense of the Patti Municipal Committee alone. In many cases, the relatives of the deceased were not informed, even though they had been identified.

Significantly, even after a complete turn-about in the law and order situation, the incidents continued, although their frequency declined. During 1994, the Patti Municipal [illegible]mmittee records show that [illegible] least 17 "unclaimed" bod[illegible] were brought by the police [illegible]cremation.

[illegible] extensive tour of the [illegible]sar district revealed that [illegible]milies of those picked [illegible] the Punjab police for [illegible]ted links with terrorists, still nurture hope of their returning home. While some families have moved habeas corpus petitions in the high court, several others have not done so for fear of police reprisals. Sources within the police disclosed that while some of the "missing" persons may have succumbed to torture by the police, some others may have been eliminated if they happened to be witnesses to these deaths in police custody.

UNDERCURRENT: While, informed political leaders acknowledge that extra-constitutional methods may have helped root out terrorism, the cost in terms of innocent lives lost appears to have been heavy. Said veteran CPI leader, Satya Pal Dang, "this has left an undercurrent of resentment in the rural areas".

The Punjab DGP, Mr K. P. S. Gill, has been maintaining that the missing youths in Punjab had gone abroad as illegal immigrants and were working there. The Additional Director General of the Punjab Police (Operations), Mr P. C. Dogra, denied any knowledge of cremations of such "unclaimed" bodies. "The state police have killed only terrorists in encounters and all these deaths have been recorded by the press as well," he added.

PLEA REJECTED: A human rights group had also compiled statistics from these municipal records and moved the high court. However, the plea was dismissed last fortnight on the ground that the affected families should be a party to the petition. A visit to the Amritsar and Tarn Taran cremation grounds confirmed that several hundred bodies were brought as "unclaimed" by the Punjab police and cremated at the expense of the municipal committees of these towns as well. Police records show that some of them were subsequently "identified" for claiming the "unannounced rewards".

Some citizens of Patti town claimed that at times they had to arrange for more wood to take care of the smouldering bodies on the cremation grounds as often the wood fell short due to the large number of unclaimed bodies coming in. These bodies were brought to Patti from various villages under the Valtoha, Bhikiwind, Harike, Kairon and Khalra police stations.

In Amritsar, Baba Bhut Nath who lights the funeral pyres at the Durgiana Mandir crematorium said that during 1992 and 1993, often five or six unclaimed bodies brought in on a single day. According to the Tarn Taran crematorium staff during 1992-1993, sometimes seven or eight unclaimed bodies were cremated in a day.

CONTRADICTORY: During 1992, the Amritsar Municipal Corporation paid for the cremation of 300 "unclaimed" bodies of youths. Sources in these municipal committees disclose that all these payments have been made by cheque and this evidence exists in the records of the banks as well. In a few cases the relatives of the "unclaimed" deceased managed to get information about the death in custody. They then contacted the cremation staff on their own and made payments for a "better" funeral.

Surprisingly while the police have submitted in writing that these persons were unidentified or unclaimed, their names and the villages they hail from are mentioned in the list. A visit to some of these villages by an Indian Express team showed that some youths had actually been picked up by the police from there.

The Indian Express, February 3, 1995

last rites nor complete official duties such as the transfer of bank accounts or properties. Most of those families had lost their heads of household and had no financial support coming in.

Jaswant and Jaspal demanded accountability of the state and asked for a response to their findings. They demanded that the wrongdoing of the Punjab Police be thoroughly investigated by the Central Bureau of Investigation (CBI), India's premier investigative agency, under the judicial scrutiny of the high court. They also asked for an investigation into other methods of secretly disposing of bodies, such as dumping them in the rivers and canals of Punjab.

This level of substantiated claims and public questioning came as a shock to the government, especially at a time when most were terrified to speak out and feared for their lives. The media widely covered the press conference. Around the world, people were stunned that Jaswant and Jaspal had shown the courage to speak out against the state with such conviction, confidence, and clarity, and absolutely no fear for their lives.

They directly accused the Director General of Police (DGP), K.P.S. Gill as responsible. He was infuriated.

Jaswant Singh demanding CBI inquiry for mass cremation cases at Punjab & Haryana High Court, Chandigarh, 1994 - Ram Narayan Kumar Collection

The State Retaliates

On January 18, 1995, K.P.S. Gill held his own press conference in Amritsar to refute the allegations made by Jaswant and his companions.

K.P.S. Gill accused the human rights organizations in Punjab of being supporters of the terrorists and insurgents. He told the media that the thousands of missing persons were Sikh youth who had left for foreign countries under fake names and with false documents, and that there were no state killings or fake encounters.

He evaded questions asked by Jaswant and his team, and he blamed Pakistani agencies and Sikh organizations from foreign countries for reviving militancy in Punjab. He had no explanation as to why thousands of bodies had been brought by the police to be cremated. He had no explanation as to why the law had been broken in following the due process of identifying the bodies or why the state was cremating them instead of handing the bodies over to their families.

The next day, January 19, Jaswant and his team called a press conference in Amritsar to challenge the claims of K.P.S. Gill. Jaswant offered to provide evidence that the bodies of persons cremated were indeed those of the disappeared persons who had been murdered in state custody and whose deaths had been faked as police encounters. He challenged K.P.S. Gill to an open debate.

Soon after these press conferences, the government brought back Ajit Singh Sandhu as the Senior Superintendent of Police (SSP) in Tarn Taran, a man notorious for exercising brute force against

SUPREME COURT OF INDIA
SUPREME COURT OF INDIA
CWP-990-1995
J.S. DHILLON
VS.
STATE OF PUNJAB

(16) THE TRIBUNE, THURSDAY, JANUARY 19, 1995

'Missing persons' not killed: Gill

From Our Correspondent

AMRITSAR, Jan 18 – The government is seized with the problem of thousands of Sikh youth, who had gone to foreign countries under fake names and documents, and were claimed as "missing persons killed by security forces in encounters," the Director-General of the Punjab police, Mr K.P.S. Gill, said here today.

Talking to newspersons, he said there was a lot of confusion as the police had made lists of the missing persons. In most of the cases, the reports were not true as the persons were missing with the consent of their parents and relatives. Their whereabouts were known to their families. He cited an example of a so-called missing person who had performed the wedding of his daughter and got his father treated at a posh hospital.

Mr Gill said it was difficult to ascertain whether these Sikh youth had gone to foreign countries on their ... by changing their names and addresses, he added.

Referring to the situation in the state, Mr Gill said the ISI of Pakistan was doing its best to revive militancy in Punjab.

He said certain Sikh "Jathebandis", staying in foreign countries, were raising funds for the militants. There had been reports that a lot of money was being collected outside for granting "Pensions" to the militant families, however, a major chunk of this money was being utilised by these organisations themselves, he added.

Mr Gill said the police had evolved a programme to improve its image. This was decided at a meeting of police officials held yesterday at Ludhiana.

Mr Gill said he was going around various districts of Punjab to emphasise on the quality of investigations.

He said stress would be laid on the constant monitoring of the cases pending for investigation. Prompt documentation would be done "since ... ing cases.

Mr Gill claimed that the figures of murders and attempts to murder cases were low as compared to the past three years.

Mr Gill said the police continued to have interaction with panchayats and students as this was necessary to improve the image of the police.

Expressing satisfaction over these interactions, he said the idea was to remove misconceptions about the police.

Mr Gill said the police exhibition arranged at Muktsar on the occasion of "Maghi mela" last week was held keeping the idea of interaction with the masses in mind. More than 1.25 lakh persons had visited the mela, he said.

Mr Gill stated that computers were being introduced in the police force to improve its performance. Conputers would also enable senior police officials to monitor crimes in various districts of the state.

He said during the past year there had been 18 cases of arms recovery, three cases of sedition and 118 cases were registered under Arms Act. As many as 76 terrorists had been killed in the state last year.

Excerpts from the hand written press note of Jaswant Singh Khalra

Ajnala, February 23 1995

"If the Punjab Government and the Punjab Police believe that by killing me and making my body disappear they can cover up the matter relating to the mass disappearance of the 25,000 "Lawaris (unclaimed)" bodies then they are mistaken because the facts relating to this matter have been disclosed to various human rights organizations throughout the world and yesterday (February 22) the Chairman of the Human Rights Wing, Jaspal Singh Dhillon has left for Manila, Philippines, to obtain international support and to participate in the World Human Rights Conference."

... I want to make it very clear to the Punjab Government and the Punjab Police that we have all the evidence, including signatures of the involved police officers, that link them to the disappearances of unclaimed bodies and we are fully prepared to present this evidence to the legal courts. For the sake of humanity, I would like to appeal to the police officers, who are eager to take my life, that I am not doing this work for compensation or due to any hatred against the police but according to the way of Gurmat (Sikh faith)."

- Jaswant Singh Khalra

suspected militants and known to have been responsible for many disappearances in the area.

Jaswant began to receive phone calls at home day and night, call after call containing abusive language threatening to kill him and harm his family. The family was sleepless and terrified as they knew that the calls were from the police. Who would they depend on to protect them if the police force itself was after their lives? Navkiran was only nine years old and Janmeet, her little brother, eight. When Jaswant was not home, the callers threatened Paramjit using foul language to describe the cruel treatment that she and her children would face if she didn't stop her husband from walking this path.

Strangers started appearing in Jaswant's neighborhood, loitering for hours, harassing and intimidating the family. The children could not go out to play, and the family began to feel imprisoned in their own home.

Several days later, Jaswant was summoned to the home of a local politician who relayed to him in person that it was in his own best interest to stop speaking out about the disappeared and against the state. In a clear threat from the state, the politician conveyed that "if the state could disappear 25,000 people, it would not hesitate to disappear 25,001."

Jaswant was distraught. Although he hid his distress from Paramjit, she knew him well enough to infer that something was wrong, and eventually he confided in her. They thought if the state had already decided to take Jaswant's life, it wouldn't matter what he did. Whether he hid at home or continued his work, it did not matter as the damage had already been done. The reports were released, and Jaswant could not take back what he knew to be true.

Together, they decided he was going to go after the state with full force. Paramjit, his best friend, his support, his partner, did not stop him; rather she gave him the strength to pursue the cause to serve his people. She reminded him that his duty as a Sikh was not only that of a father to their own children but also to seek justice for the innumerable children whose fathers and mothers had been taken away by the state.

Jaswant emerged more resolute than ever.

On February 27, 1995, Jaswant called another press conference in Amritsar publicizing the threats to his person and warned the state that eliminating him would not put an end to the matter of the 25,000 *lawaris*. He held SSP A.S. Sandhu personally responsible for over one thousand disappearances and pointed to the court cases against Sandhu regarding numerous fake encounters. Jaswant said that if something were to happen to him, Director General of Police, K.P.S. Gill and Chief Minister Beant Singh should be held directly responsible.

Soon after, Jaswant petitioned the state's high court, asking for an investigation into the disappearances and illegal cremations. The high court dismissed the petition on the grounds that it was "vague" and did not qualify for public litigation. The court said that only a disappeared individual's family could file the case and not the human rights groups.

Jaswant received the same treatment from the Supreme Court of India. He then approached the National Human Rights Commission (NHRC) of India in New Delhi, a statutory public body responsible for the protection and promotion of human rights, as embodied in international covenants and guaranteed by the Constitution of India.

He presented his case before the NHRC and pleaded for the Commission to apply pressure on the Indian judicial system to initiate inquiries into these unlawful killings. But NHRC, too, shrugged him off, showing their own helplessness by saying that Punjab state's Human Rights Commission should investigate the matter. Alas, there was no such commission.

Jaswant felt utterly frustrated as he came to the realization that obtaining justice from a system that itself perpetrated the crimes was impossible. He felt he had little time to take this evidence to the world before he, himself, was silenced for good. He also knew that while the Indian government could silence its own citizens through oppression and coercion as they were confined within India's borders, it could not muzzle humanitarians living in other countries beyond its reach.

He trusted that the Sikh diaspora which had fought for the good of all humanity and had raised its voice in defending the weak, defenseless, and voiceless, would surely raise its voice for fellow Sikhs in India. He knew that they could not be silenced once they knew the whole truth.

The Voice goes International

Between April and July of 1995, Jaswant traveled to Canada, Austria, and England to inform local and international human rights groups about the disappearances in Punjab. He met with many people, politicians, and organizations to request that they ask the government of India to seriously investigate the matter of custodial tortures, forced disappearances, killings, and illegal cremations carried out by the security forces in Punjab.

On June 1, 1995, Jaswant was invited to speak at the Canadian Parliament in Ottawa in a visit organized by the Sikh advocacy group, the World Sikh Organization. Addressing a large group of parliamentarians, he spoke of the ongoing genocide of the Sikhs in India, providing data and evidence to back up his claims. He expressed frustration at his failure to procure an inquiry let alone justice for the thousands of innocents murdered by the state.

He applauded the Canadians for coming such a long way in safeguarding human rights and setting an example for the rest of the world. He marveled at the changes that had taken place since the time his grandfather, Harnam Singh, had not been allowed in this very land, where he, himself, now spoke before Parliament.

Sikh-Canadians had been contributing citizens of Canada for almost a century, and their families back home were facing oppression. Jaswant appealed to the Canadian Parliament and to the people of Canada to stand up for the human rights of Sikhs in India.

Jaswant Singh speaking at the Canadian parliamentary dinner hosted by the W.S.O., June 1995 - Family collection

Jaswant's speech at the Gurdwara Ontario Khalsa Darbar in Toronto on Vaisakhi of April 1995 is legendary. It has been an inspiration to legions of human rights activists. He said:

"Thousands of mothers await their children even though some may know that the oppressor has not spared their lives on this earth. A mother's heart is such that even if she sees her child's dead body, she does not accept that her child has left her. And those mothers who have not even seen their children's corpses, they were asking us: at least find out, is our child alive or not?"

"It has been a mockery of the law. It is a mockery of the entire Sikh community. It is a mockery of the families who only wanted to know if their children have been killed in custody or are still alive and who only demanded the death certificates of their loved ones."

"We will seek justice in the highest courts, but higher than those courts is the court of people. And in the court of people, we want to tell the whole world that you called us terrorists, you called us separatists, but dear people, the ones you called messengers of peace and apostles of democracy – please know their truth – and then tell us who is the terrorist and who is the truthful."

He appealed to the Sikhs in the Diaspora to contribute to the fight for the rights of their brothers and sisters back home. At the minimum, he told them, they should ensure that the data, including the exact count and details of the disappeared, be documented in its entirety.

"We say that we have been wronged, and that much cruelty has been inflicted upon us, but we have not learnt how to keep and

Jaswant Singh sharing details of mass cremation cases in Punjab with British politicians, London, 1995 - Family collection

convey the account of the oppression. Sometimes we say about fifty thousand were disappeared and sometimes we say about one million. We lose credibility for our cause by not giving the world the exact figures and substantiated data. So I say, you all must take this initiative of accounting as your own business, because it is not only the issue of the families whose members were disappeared, it is a matter of all the Sikh people, nay... it is a matter of entire humanity..."

Jaswant's trip and public engagements did much to highlight the human rights abuses in Punjab. Despite escalating threats, and his well-wishers' attempts to stop him from going back, he returned to Punjab on July 26, 1995. He knew that he had angered the government with his activism and by publicizing its crimes against the Sikhs.

After his return, Jaswant could not afford to waste even a minute. He learned that the police was already intimidating the families who had filed cases of disappearances in the High Court. The police was threatening them of dire consequences if the cases were not withdrawn. In several cases, elderly family members of the disappeared were picked up by the police and disappeared after they filed court cases.

Jaswant immediately launched a press campaign and exposed the Tarn Taran police officials' terror tactics against victims' families. A front page story by *The Ajit*, a leading daily newspaper of Punjab, revealed the terror tactics of the police not only against the general public but also against honest police employees who failed to comply with the department orders regarding enforced-state-terrorism. The story greatly infuriated SSP A.S. Sandhu.

The police responded with a press release of their own, stating that Jaswant Singh was a member of a militant organization called the Khalistan Commando Force and the Naxalite movement, acting on the instructions of "India's foreign enemies" to destabilize the peaceful environment of Punjab. They also claimed that the alleged disappeared had escaped across the border to Pakistan and were living there.

Meanwhile, Jaswant's international campaign had been generating more action, and several congressmen in the U.S., as well as members of parliament in Canada and the U.K. pressed their governments to investigate India's human rights abuses in Punjab.

Indian intelligence agencies interrogated Jaswant and all those with whom he interacted locally and internationally. He and his family were threatened and intimidated even more than before, and his every move was monitored.

Friends urged Jaswant to leave Amritsar and go into hiding for his own safety, but he continued to work on many crucial cases to give a voice to the innocent. To his mind, this was the only way to assure that more lives would not be lost. As the clock ticked on, he kept his focus on his objectives rather than worrying about his own life. He had already left once to save his life but had returned to Punjab despite the danger. He knew what was in store for him but was determined never to leave again.

The Inevitable

On August 31, 1995, Beant Singh, Punjab's Chief Minister, who had led a brutal counter-insurgency campaign, endorsing all human rights abuses and terror tactics in Punjab and enjoying the maximum possible security in the country, was assassinated near his office in Chandigarh by a powerful bomb. The blast also took the lives of seventeen members of his security team and his young assassin Dilawar Singh, an ex-police Constable who had decided to put an end to the state brutalities by sending a strong message to the government.

Babbar Khalsa International (BKI), a militant Khalistani organization, claimed responsibility. The security forces immediately launched a vengeful campaign throughout Punjab, killing many young people suspected of ties to BKI, and arresting and torturing many others in an attempt to track down the assassins.

Jaswant feared that his enemies within the police force, those whom he had made uncomfortable, would take advantage of the situation to try to implicate him in the conspiracy of the assassination.

While his family feared for his safety, Jaswant learned that his father, Bapu Kartar Singh, had fallen ill in the village.

Bapu-ji and *Maañ-Ji* had been restless and frightened ever since their son had taken up the cause of exposing the secret cremations. They knew that it could cost Jaswant his life. *Bapu-ji*'s health had been steadily failing as he worried about his beloved son. He became especially anxious and ill after a secret visit from a sub-

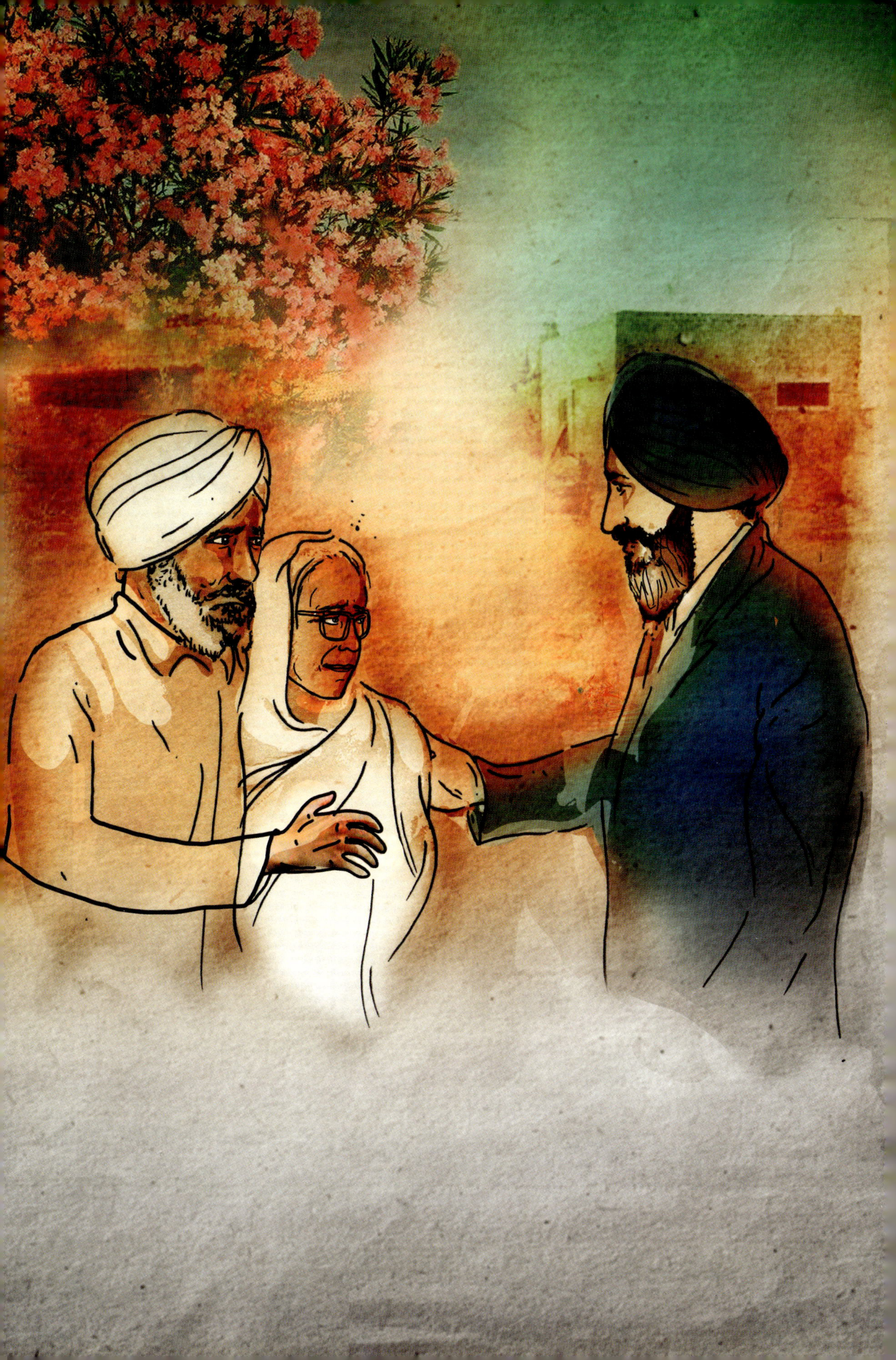

Bapu-ji Kartar Singh and Maañ-Ji Mukhtiar Kaur, Khalra, 2005
- Family collection

inspector of the local police station in the last week of August 1995. This officer had once been *Bapu-ji*'s dear student and seemed genuinely concerned about Jaswant's life. He requested that *Bapu-ji* ask Jaswant to be very careful and said that his police station had received informal instructions to pick Jaswant up without a legal arrest warrant whenever Jaswant visited next. It was for this reason that *Bapu-ji* did not want Jaswant to visit him.

But on Sunday, September 3, 1995, Jaswant decided to disregard his own safety and visit his parents in the village of Khalra.

This upset *Bapu-ji*, as this was how other young men and women from Punjab had been picked up, disappeared, killed, and their bodies surreptitiously disposed of. Jaswant tried to quell his father's anxiety by facing the situation head on. He went to the Khalra police station and invited the Police In-Charge to arrest him if he had the instructions to do so. The Police Inspector was embarrassed and told him that he had no probable cause or authorization to arrest him.

Still, *Bapu-ji* remained uneasy. That evening, with his voice cracking and tears rolling down his face, *Bapu-ji* asked his beloved son why he had chosen to invite death and trouble on the family by taking up the issue of secret cremations. Jaswant replied, "Father, everyone has to die when the time comes. I could die in my bed, in an accident, or as a martyr for the cause. I choose the latter." *Bapu-ji* was speechless. He embraced his son and blessed him. He felt enormous pride in his son's character and integrity.

Maañ-Ji, Mukhtiar Kaur, embraced him and asked him when he would return. "I will keep coming back," Jaswant told her.

The next afternoon, Jaswant Singh left for Amritsar after saying goodbye to his parents. They held each other for a long time, somehow knowing that this would be their last embrace.

Jaswant Singh Khalra at Darbar Sahib Amritsar, 1994 - Family collection

The 25,001st Disappeared

On Wednesday, September 6, 1995, the day began with the usual chores, as Paramjit made breakfast and got ready for work. Jaswant helped the children get ready for school and started watering the plants. Something occurred to him, and he left the water-hose running, found Paramjit, and asked her, "You will be able to educate the children properly, won't you?"

"Am I not the one who is educating them right now?" Paramjit replied. She did not grasp the meaning of the conversation at the time.

Paramjit left for work at Guru Nanak Dev University as the children left for school. When they said goodbye to their father, Jaswant was lovingly humming a hymn from *Gurbani* that had been on his lips since that morning. It was Jaswant's habit to sing one or two random lines from *Gurbani* all day long. That day, it was *Dubidha door karho liv laai...*, which meant, "Please remove my duality; let me be connected to you..."

Jaswant Singh received Rajiv Singh Randhawa, a journalist from *The Ajit*, at his home. While they waited for another journalist from the *Indian Express*, Jaswant stepped outside to wash his car, getting it ready to go to Tarn Taran for some disappearance interviews. It was at about 9:20 a.m. as he washed his car that he was picked up by armed commandos of the security forces outside his home in a blue van accompanied by a police jeep.

Rajiv Singh Randhawa and another neighbor, Sukhraj Kaur, witnessed the abduction. They called the university and left a message for Paramjit. She returned immediately and found the water hose that Jaswant used to wash the car still running. They contacted the police station, but the police denied having arrested Jaswant.

Upon their return from school, the children learned that their father had been picked up by the police. They were scared, and they asked their mother if their father had done something wrong. Paramjit didn't know how to respond as she held them close to her heart. She knew that the rest of her life would be an uphill battle, and she had to be strong. The fight against the state had now fallen on her shoulders, along with the care and education of the two terrified children, only nine and ten years old.

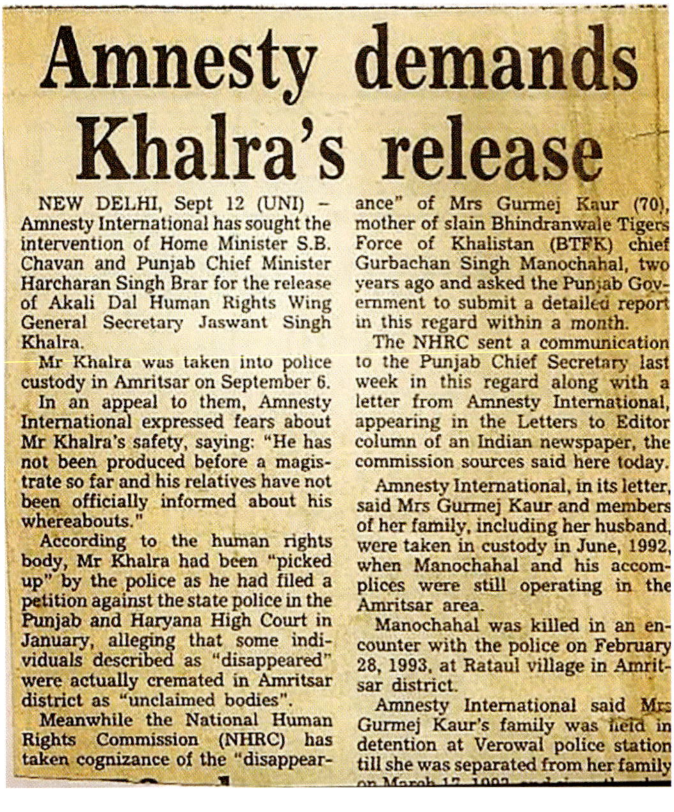

Amnesty demands Khalra's release

NEW DELHI, Sept 12 (UNI) – Amnesty International has sought the intervention of Home Minister S.B. Chavan and Punjab Chief Minister Harcharan Singh Brar for the release of Akali Dal Human Rights Wing General Secretary Jaswant Singh Khalra.

Mr Khalra was taken into police custody in Amritsar on September 6.

In an appeal to them, Amnesty International expressed fears about Mr Khalra's safety, saying: "He has not been produced before a magistrate so far and his relatives have not been officially informed about his whereabouts."

According to the human rights body, Mr Khalra had been "picked up" by the police as he had filed a petition against the state police in the Punjab and Haryana High Court in January, alleging that some individuals described as "disappeared" were actually cremated in Amritsar district as "unclaimed bodies".

Meanwhile the National Human Rights Commission (NHRC) has taken cognizance of the "disappearance" of Mrs Gurmej Kaur (70), mother of slain Bhindranwale Tigers Force of Khalistan (BTFK) chief Gurbachan Singh Manochahal, two years ago and asked the Punjab Government to submit a detailed report in this regard within a month.

The NHRC sent a communication to the Punjab Chief Secretary last week in this regard along with a letter from Amnesty International, appearing in the Letters to Editor column of an Indian newspaper, the commission sources said here today.

Amnesty International, in its letter, said Mrs Gurmej Kaur and members of her family, including her husband, were taken in custody in June, 1992, when Manochahal and his accomplices were still operating in the Amritsar area.

Manochahal was killed in an encounter with the police on February 28, 1993, at Rataul village in Amritsar district.

Amnesty International said Mrs Gurmej Kaur's family was held in detention at Verowal police station till she was separated from her family

The Indian Express,
September 13, 1995

INDIA: FEAR OF DISAPPEARANCE / FEAR OF TORTURE: JASWANT SINGH KHALRA, HUMAN RIGHTS ACTIVIST

7 September 1995, Index number: ASA 20/026/1995

Jaswant Singh Khalra, General Secretary of the Human Rights Wing of the Akali Dal political party, has not been seen since 6 September 1995, when he was arrested by police outside his home. In January 1995 his party filed a petition in the Punjab and Haryana high Court concerning the deaths of hundreds of unidentified individuals. Shortly after the filing of this petition Jaswant Singh Khalra was reportedly threatened by a member of the Punjab Police. AI is concerned for his safety.

UNITED KINGDOM: WRONGFUL DETENTION OF ASYLUM-SEEKER RAGHBIR SINGH

1 February 1996, Index number: EUR 45/001/1996

Since 1983, thousands of suspected members and supporters of Sikh opposition groups advocating the creation of a separate Sikh state (Khalistan) in Punjab have been arrested by the Indian security forces and detained under special legislation suspending normal legal safeguards. In many cases the arrest of the detainees has remained unacknowledged for weeks or months, and there have been numerous reports of torture during interrogation. Scores of those arrested have been tortured to death or have otherwise been deliberately and unlawfully killed in custody (although official reports sometimes say they have died in 'encounters' with the police or while 'trying to escape'), while others have simply 'disappeared', the security forces refusing to acknowledge that they had ever been arrested.

The Lamp Extinguished

Jaswant Singh's disappearance made headlines. While his organization, now led by his wife, knocked at the doors of the police and the courts, he was moved from one police station to another, interrogated, threatened, and tortured in secret.

Approximately forty-eight days after his abduction, Jaswant was taken to the Jhabal police station, where he was continuously tortured by senior police officials, including SSP A.S. Sandhu, for four more days under the pretext of interrogation. At Jhabal, a Special Police Officer (SPO), Kuldip Singh, in charge of his custody, kept account of all those who visited and participated in interrogations and torture with all the details.

One evening, SPO Kuldip Singh was asked to take Jaswant Singh to SSP A.S. Sandhu's house in Manavala village near Amritsar, where DGP K.P.S. Gill, along with another senior officer, interrogated and tortured him in retaliation for his activism.

On October 28, 1995, after fifty-two days of illegal detention and torture, Jaswant Singh was shot dead at approximately 7 p.m. in the presence of multiple police officers at the Jhabal Police Station. His body was dismembered and dumped the same night into the Harike Canal – the very canal that Jaswant had been watching for the dead bodies of the disappeared.

SSP A.S Sandhu and the officials who participated in Jaswant Singh's torture and execution then met at the Irrigation Department's guest house at Harike for a celebration over drinks, as testified by the SPO Kuldip Singh three years later.

KPS GILL
AS SANDHU

Jaswant Singh Khalra was silenced forever, but he had accomplished what he had come to do on this earth. He began the methodical and meticulous documentation of human rights abuses in Punjab so that the whole world could see the truth. The government believed that by silencing Jaswant Singh, they would eliminate all voices who dared to challenge the state and its evil doings, but they had not known that Jaswant Singh was a lamp who had lit many others in his short life, and it would be impossible to keep the world in darkness for long.

Harike Pattan, a barrage, reservoir, and wetland at the confluence of the rivers Beas and Satluj (Sutlej). Here, the bodies of Jaswant Singh and others illegally murdered by security forces were disposed of. It feeds the longest and one of the largest canals in India – the Indira Gandhi Canal. It travels some 400 miles carrying water to Rajasthan. From here on, Satluj flows as a mere stream for a short distance and enters West Punjab.

ਜਸਵੰਤ ਸਿੰਘ ਖਾਲੜਾ

(ਸਫਾ 1 ਦੀ ਬਾਕੀ)

ਮਾਰਚ, 1998 ਨੂੰ ਪੰਜਾਬ ਦੇ ਡਾਇਰੈਕਟਰ ਜਨਰਲ ਪੁਲਿਸ ਸ੍ਰੀ ਪੀ. ਸੀ. ਡੋਗਰਾ ਵੱਲ ਭੇਜਿਆ ਉਹ ਪੱਤਰ ਵੀ ਦਿਖਾਇਆ, ਜਿਸ ਵਿਚ ਕਿਹਾ ਗਿਆ ਸੀ ਕਿ ਸੁਪਰੀਮ ਕੋਰਟ ਵੱਲੋਂ ਗਵਾਹ ਦੀ ਸੁਰੱਖਿਆ ਦੀ ਅਹਿਮੀਅਤ ਵੇਖਦਿਆਂ ਹੋਇਆ ਦਿੱਤੇ ਗਏ ਨਿਰਦੇਸ਼ਾਂ ਮੁਤਾਬਿਕ ਕੁਲਦੀਪ ਸਿੰਘ ਨੂੰ ਸੀ. ਆਰ. ਪੀ. ਐਫ. ਦੀ ਸੁਰੱਖਿਆ ਦਿੱਤੀ ਜਾਵੇ। ਕੁਲਦੀਪ ਨੇ ਕਿਹਾ ਕਿ ਸੁਪਰੀਮ ਕੋਰਟ ਦੇ ਹੁਕਮਾਂ ਦੇ ਨਾ ਮੰਨਣ ਕਰਕੇ ਹੀ ਪੰਜਾਬ ਪੁਲਿਸ ਉਸ ਵੱਲੋਂ ਬੀਬੀ ਪਰਮਜੀਤ ਕੌਰ ਖਾਲੜਾ ਦੇ ਖਿਲਾਫ ਸ਼ਾਹਕੋਟ ਥਾਣੇ 'ਚ ਰਿਸ਼ਵਤ ਦੇ

ਖਾਲੜਾ ਅਗਵਾ ਕਾਂਡ ਦਾ ਚਰਚਿਤ ਗਵਾਹ ਐਸ ਪੀ. ਓ. ਕੁਲਦੀਪ ਸਿੰਘ। ਫੋਟੋ: ਸੁਖਦੀਪ ਸਿੰ

ਜਸਵੰਤ ਸਿੰਘ ਖਾਲੜਾ ਨੂੰ ਮੇਰੇ ਸਾਹਮਣੇ ਮਾਰਿਆ

ਸੁਖਦੀਪ ਸਿੰਘ ਸਿੱਧੂ

ਵਿਖੇ ਸਾਰੇ ਬਿਆਨ ਕਲਮਬੰਦ ਕਰਾ ਚੁੱਕਾ ਹੈ, ਜਿਸ ਤੋਂ ਬਾਅਦ ਪੰਜਾਬ ਪੁਲਿਸ ਦੇ ਡੀ. ਜੀ. ਪੀ. ਸਮੇਤ ਸਮੇਤ ਕਈ ਉੱਚ ਅਧਿਕਾਰੀ ਮੇਰੇ ਵੱਲੋਂ ਸੀ. ਆਰ. ਪੀ. ਐਫ. ਦੀ ਸੁਰੱਖਿਆ ਛਤਰੀ ਦੇਣ ਬਾਰੇ ਕੀਤੀਆਂ

duty in view of the model code of conduct and the ban imposed by the commission ... in his written statement that Ms Wadhwa was removed ... tioned before the Bench tomorrow. ... Sources in the administra- ... issuance of revised proce-

K.P.S. Gill visited Khalra in confinement, says witness

Recounts tale of police brutality before his 'murder'

Jangveer Singh
Tribune News Service

Patiala, February 16

The disappearance of human rights activist Jaswant Singh Khalra has taken a new turn with the sole witness who claims to have witnessed the murder of the activist, alleging that he had seen former Punjab Police Director-General of Police K.P.S. Gill go into a room in which Khalra was being kept at Manawala in Taran Tarn.

The witness, Kuldeep Singh, is a former Special Police Officer who claims he was recruited into the police by former Taran Tarn Senior Superintendent of Police Ajit Singh Sandhu. He told the cour of the Additional Sessions Judge here that it was Sandhu's house in Manawala village in Taran Tarn which was visited by K.P.S. Gill and other "clean shaven official" a few days before Khalra was murdered in 1995.

The witness who told TNS after stepping out of the court that he was happy he had finally been able to tell the truth, said during his deposition that he was taken to the residence of the Taran Tarn, SSP, by Jhabal Police Station SHO Satnam Singh who was keeping Khalra locked in illegal confinement. He further alleged that Mr K.P.S. Gill remained in the oom where Khalra was eing kept for half an hour adding that during the journey back to the Jhabal police station, SHO Satnam Singh told Khalra that he would have saved himself if he had listened to the "advice" of the DGP.

Giving a lengthy deposition, the former SPO said he came into contact with Mr Ajit Singh Sandhu, who was a prime accused in the Khalra disappearance case before he committed suicide in 1994. He said when Sandhu was posted to Taran Tarn in 1995 he accompanied him as a gun man.

The witness said he was posted to the Jhabal police station in the police district subsequently and it was here that he was handed over the keys of a room in which Khalra was being kept.

The SPO said his responsibility was to provide food to Khalra and it was during this time that DSP Jaspal Singh and his body guard Arvinder besides Sarhali SHO Surinderpal Singh, Manochahal SHO Jasbir Singh, Prithipal Singh and Balwinder Singh Gora came to the police station in separate cars.

He alleged that the police officials started beating up Khalra and "I was asked to get a glass of hot water by SHO Satnam Singh".

The SPO said even as he was heating up the water he heard the sound of two shots and when he rushed towards the room, he was told by Satnam Singh to go where the cars were parked.

"Subsequently Balwinder Singh Gora reversed the Maruti van in which he had come and he and Arvinder took hold of Khalra's legs and arms to dump him into the boot of the vehicle. I saw blood oozing out of Khalra's chest," he claimed. Kuldeep said while he sat in SHO Satnam Singh's vehicle the two other cars containing the same police officials moved ahead.

At around 10 pm the cavalcade reached Harike where Arvinder and Balwinder Singh Gora took out Khalra's body and threw it into a canal, he alleged.

Telling a gory tale of brutality, the SPO alleg that all cars proceeded the Harike guest hou after the act where oth police officials, inclu ing Mr Ajit Singh San hu, were present.

He said while the offic went inside he, Arvin and Balwinder were giv two bottles of liquor wh they consumed in the la of the rest house.

Kuldeep Singh said had a change of heart the issue after listening human rights acti speaking about the di pearance of Khalra decided to tell his tale has taken several yea do so during which ti have resisted severe sure from the police officia...

Coverage on S.P.O Kuldip Singh's testimonies with details on how Jaswant Singh was killed in his presence, March 1998

ਮਰਣੁ ਨ ਮੰਦਾ ਲੋਕਾ ਆਖੀਐ ਜੇ ਮਰਿ ਜਾਣੈ ਐਸਾ ਕੋਇ॥

Death would not be called bad, O people,
if one knew how to truly die.

Guru Baba Nanak, SGGS: 579

THE TORCHBEARER

The Fight for Justice

Jaswant Singh Khalra was no ordinary man. Anyone who came in contact with him was inspired. Even Paramjit, who was already an activist when she met Jaswant wasn't left untouched by his energy. Though she had a full-time job and two small children, she was not a woman who could be silenced by the state.

Now that her beloved partner, friend, husband, and "The Leader" was gone, Jaswant's mission became her mission. She would leave no stone unturned, and her first goal was to locate Jaswant.

On September 6, 1995, following Jaswant Singh's abduction, Paramjit Kaur, along with a key eyewitness, went to the Islamabad Police Station, Amritsar, to lodge a complaint, which the police refused to register.

On September 7, Paramjit again went to the police station with Jaswant Singh's close friends Gurbhej Singh Palasaur and Satinderpal Singh Palasaur. The police were of no help. She then went to the *Shiromani Gurudwara Prabandhak Committee* (SGPC) office in the *Darbar Sahib* complex. She met with G.S. Tohra, the then president of the organization. At her behest, G.S. Tohra sent complaints about Jaswant Singh's abduction via telegram to various government functionaries, including one to Justice Kuldip Singh, a Supreme Court judge.

Shiromani Gurudwara Prabandhak Committee: An organization that manages all the historical Gurdwaras in Punjab

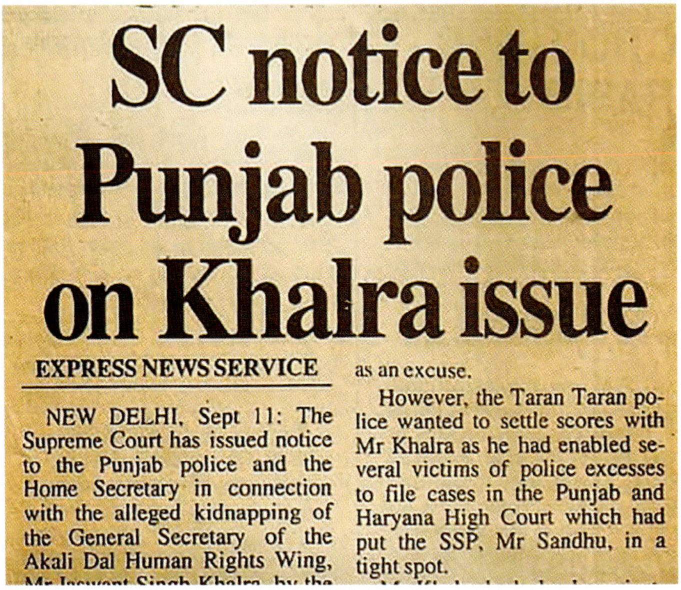
SC notice to Punjab police on Khalra issue

EXPRESS NEWS SERVICE

NEW DELHI, Sept 11: The Supreme Court has issued notice to the Punjab police and the Home Secretary in connection with the alleged kidnapping of the General Secretary of the Akali Dal Human Rights Wing,

as an excuse.

However, the Taran Taran police wanted to settle scores with Mr Khalra as he had enabled several victims of police excesses to file cases in the Punjab and Haryana High Court which had put the SSP, Mr Sandhu, in a tight spot.

The Indian Express, September 1995

On September 9, 1995, three days after the abduction, Paramjit Kaur filed a petition before the Supreme Court of India requesting that Jaswant Singh be presented before the court. The petition also gave a detailed description of the eye-witness account of his abduction.

On September 11, Justice Kuldip Singh issued a notice to the Punjab government to either produce Jaswant Singh or furnish his whereabouts within a week. The Punjab Police responded with multiple affidavits stating that it had no interest in picking Jaswant Singh up, and they denied ever threatening him or having had him in their custody.

On November 15, 1995, the Supreme Court directed the Central Bureau of Investigation (CBI), to investigate Jaswant Singh's abduction and the allegations contained in his press release dated January 16, 1995. The CBI was given three months to solve the abduction case.

On July 30, 1996, the CBI submitted a report stating that nine officers of the Punjab Police, acting on the orders of SSP A.S. Sandhu, had been responsible for Jaswant Singh's abduction and disappearance. The Supreme Court directed the CBI to initiate a prosecution on charges of conspiracy and kidnapping. At that time, the court had no knowledge of Jaswant Singh's murder by the police. Hence, the charges of kidnapping with the intent to secretly confine a person were not enough to keep A.S. Sandhu and others in custody.

While the courts moved at their own pace, Paramjit Kaur, aided by other human rights activists, did everything in her power to speak out about Jaswant Singh's disappearance. Like the families of thousands that had disappeared before, she was unsure if her husband was alive or dead.

On May 24, 1997, SSP A.S. Sandhu reportedly committed suicide by throwing himself in front of a moving train near Mohali. A.S. Sandhu had been imprisoned for several months prior to that on charges involving the illegal abduction, torture, and custodial death of Kuljit Singh Dhat, a relative of Bhagat Singh, the famous pre-independence freedom fighter and hero of Jaswant's. The note that A.S. Sandhu left behind said, "It is better to die than to live in shame."

Soon after the death of A.S. Sandhu, SPO Kuldip Singh, who held Jaswant Singh in custody during his last days, heard Paramjit Kaur speak at a public meeting on human rights abuses in Punjab. Paramjit was working relentlessly to find answers about Jaswant's abduction and other abductions that the court had ordered. Balwinder Singh, a former head constable from Jhabal who had become a human rights activist, also spoke at the meeting.

Kuldip had been wanting to testify to the truth but feared for his life while A.S. Sandhu was alive. After hearing Paramjit speak, he decided that he could no longer remain silent as the world deserved to know what the state had done to Jaswant Singh. He gathered his courage and privately met with Balwinder Singh. He told him all that he knew of Jaswant Singh's killing and the disposal of his body. Paramjit Kaur and Balwinder Singh contacted the CBI officers investigating the case, who then invited Kuldip Singh to Delhi to make a formal statement. Despite threats on his life, Kuldip Singh offered his formal statement to the CBI on March 2, 1998. His testimony provided the breakthrough that led to convictions in the case.

It took Paramjit Kaur and her organization, the Khalra Action Committee, ten long years to procure justice for Jaswant Singh's abduction and murder. She and the five closest friends of Jaswant Singh, Gurbhej Singh Palasaur, Satinderpal Singh Palasaur, Dalbir Singh Pattarkar, Sukhwinder Singh Gill, and Harmandeep Singh Sarhali, left no stone unturned in their effort to find him. They went from police station to police station as they heard rumors or information of Jaswant Singh's custody. After they learned of his murder, they spent most of their hard-earned money commuting to endless court hearings, pursuing the extremely slow-moving proceedings.

On November 18, 2005, six Punjab Police officials were convicted and sentenced by the CBI court. Two were given life terms and four others were sentenced to seven years of imprisonment. In 2007, the Punjab and Haryana High Court changed the sentence; five of the six convicted were given life sentences and one was released. SPO Kuldip Singh's testimony also implicated K.P.S. Gill in Jaswant

Singh's disappearance and murder. Despite that, no charges were brought against him. Kuldip Singh died under mysterious circumstances in October 2011.

Khalra's wife unhappy over verdict

TRIBUNE NEWS SERVICE

PATIALA, NOVEMBER 18

With the indictment of Punjab Police personnel involved in the disappearance of her husband Jaswant Singh Khalra, Paramjit Kaur Khalra is a relieved women. She is not happy with the quantum of the punishment but feels her husband's work and their efforts to unmask the unlawful working of the Punjab Police have borne fruit.

"Today's verdict has proved that these people were behind the disappearance of my husband and his murder. It has brought to the fore the black deeds of the police. Since my husband was working on unmasking the fake encounters, they planned to eliminating him."

The case has been an emotional rollercoaster ride for her family. "I am not emotional about it any more. Ten years we have struggled to get justice for my husband

Paramjit Kaur Khalra with her counsel Brijinder Singh Sodhi at District Courts in Patiala on Friday. Photo: Rajesh Sachar

The Tribune, November 2005

In July 1996, the Supreme Court ordered India's National Human Rights Commission (NHRC) to address all cases related to mass cremations and granted extraordinary powers to the commission to complete its task. However, in over ten years of proceedings, the NHRC failed to properly address even a single case.

Paramjit succeeded in attaining closure and justice for her husband's murder, but she did not stop there. Through her guidance and leadership, the organization she co-founded, the Khalra Mission Organization, was eventually successful in its fight to secure monetary compensation for the victims' families. Through her co-

Convict Gill for murder: Paramjit Khalra

EXPRESS NEWS SERVICE
JALANDHAR, DECEMBER 10

Urges CBI to present supplementary challan against Gill in CBI court

PARAMJIT Kaur Khalra, widow of deceased human rights activist Jaswant Singh Khalra, today demanded that the CBI present a supplementary challan against former director general of police (DGP), Punjab, K.P.S. Gill in the CBI court. She also demanded that Gill should be convicted in the murder case of her husband, as he was responsible for his death.

Talking to mediapersons, Paramjit, accompanied by her lawyer Rajwinder Singh Bains and members of the Khalra Mission Committee, said the main witness in her husband's murder case, SPO Kuldip Singh, had mentioned in his statement in

Paramjit Khalra with her lawyer and members of the Khalra Mission Committee in Jalandhar. ***Sarabjit Singh***

the then DGP, K.P.S. Gill, had himself interrogated Khalra for 45 minutes.

Singh, the CBI should present a challan against Gill.

"I will wait for three

directions to CBI to present a challan against Gill in the CBI court," she said. She also appealed to the CBI to file an application in the High Court against the CBI court's recent decision so that all the six accused convicted in the case could be given life sentences. Presently, only two have been convicted for life, while four have got away with only seven years' RI.

Khalra Mission Committee members said they will set up a memorial of Jaswant Singh Khalra on the samadhi of former Punjab chief minister Beant Singh in Chandigarh and a Sikh shahidi minar in the memory of Sikhs killed in the 1984 riots near the samadhis of Rajiv Gandhi and Indira Gandhi in Delhi, be-

The Indian Express, December 2007

petitioning, close to two thousand families from Amritsar and the present Tarn Taran districts have been able to receive compensation for the disappeared despite many legal hurdles. Her ongoing fight for justice has resulted in the conviction of several senior police officers for the cases of forced disappearances.

Most importantly, her non-stop activism has made it impossible to deny the reality of thousands of disappearances and extrajudicial executions. As a result of the convictions and sentencing in Jaswant Singh's case and through the compensation for the 2,097 individuals illegally cremated in Amritsar, the government has admitted to gross human rights violations in Punjab. Paramjit's fight, however, is far from over. Thousands of families who still have no information on the fate of their disappeared family members await justice.

Khalra case: key witness found dead

MYSTERY Ex-SPO Kuldip Singh feared for his life as he had blamed former DGP KPS Gill for activist's disappearance, 'murder'

HT Correspondent
chdnewsdesk@hindustantimes.com

TARN TARAN: Special police officer (SPO) Kuldip Singh, a key witness in the case pertaining to the disappearance of human rights activist Jaswant Singh Khalra, was found dead in his house at Bacchhre village in the district on Thursday.

Kuldip's wife, in her statement to the police, stated that when she went to his room in the morning, she found him lying unconscious. She called the personnel deputed for his security. They took him to the civil hos- … group, was present.

A panel of three doctors conducted the post-mortem, following which the body was handed over to his family. The doctors' report is awaited.

Family sources said Kuldip had been upset for the past three months. He had even gone missing from home, but was traced soon by the Batala police and brought back to the village.

About 10 CRPF jawans had been deployed for his security after he expressed the apprehension that he could be harmed as he had named former DGP KPS Gill as being behind

Crucial testimony

Kuldip Singh was an SPO (special police officer) during the days of militancy. He was said to have been close to then Tarn Taran SSP Ajit Singh Sandhu. He had told the CBI court that the police had tortured Jaswant Singh Khalra and thrown his body into the river at Harike. His statement led to the court awarding 20 years imprisonment to all seven con-

Khalra had allegedly found out that a large number of unidentified bodies had been cremated by the Punjab Police after "fake" encounters in the border districts. He was allegedly abducted from his house on September 5, 1995.
The Khalra disappearance case was probed by the CBI on directions of the Punjab and Haryana high

The Hindustan Times, October 2011

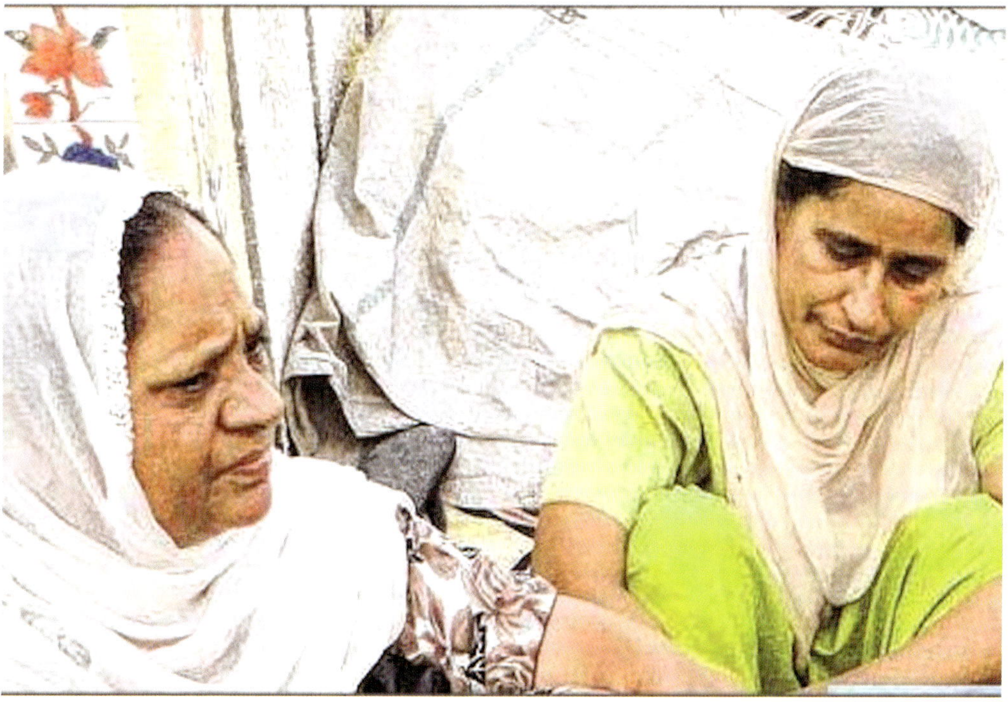

Paramjit Kaur with S.P.O Kuldip Singh's wife - Kanwaljit Kaur, after his death, Tarn Taran, October 2011

Epilogue

The Fight Continues

Maañ-Ji, Mukhtiar Kaur, the proverbial 25,001st mother of Punjab, whose son disappeared, hoped for her people to follow in the footsteps of her son, Jaswant Singh Khalra, and to uphold the dignity of Human Rights for all. She believed that her son's last words to her, "I will keep coming back," meant so. She passed away on November 25, 2009.

Bapu-ji, Kartar Singh said in an interview, "My son followed the path of truth and bold opposition to injustice. He was proud of his ancestral history of martyrdom for justice and freedom. In spite of my personal grief at his loss, I know that if there is to be any hope for Punjab and for India there has to be a resurgence of that spirit of freedom and the courage of conviction which my son embodied. In spite of the rotten state of affairs today, I have faith that there will be a new phase of struggle to realize the ideals of freedom which our leaders have betrayed. I hope Jaswant's sacrifice would contribute to initiating that process." Kartar Singh died on December 13, 2010 still awaiting justice.

Citizens for Democracy reported on Punjab, "It was a terrible tale of sadistic torture, ruthless killings, fake encounters, calculated ill-treatment of women and children, and corruption and graft on a large scale." The state of those parents who still await justice is evident in this testimony from Mohinder Singh, the father of an extrajudicial execution victim, Jugraj Singh:

"I did everything in the pursuit of truth and justice. I even begged. But all this failed me. What else could I have done... There is a Punjabi saying that after twelve years, even a pile of manure gets to be heard. But for me, after twelve years, nobody is listening. This must mean that I am worth even less than manure."

Ram Narayan Kumar, a human rights activist from Andhra Pradesh, India, moved by the plight of Punjab, dedicated much of his life to documenting widespread human rights violations in the state. A Reuters Foundation fellow at the University of Oxford, Kumar spent several years researching, interviewing, and writing books on the Sikh struggle and state terror. His joint work, *Reduced To Ashes,* a compilation of about 600 cases of human rights violations in the state, highlighting the work and life of Jaswant Singh Khalra, was instrumental in prompting the National Human Rights Commission to take notice of the large scale custodial disappearances and extra-judicial killings in Punjab.

In keeping with the vision of Jaswant Singh to document the state crimes in Punjab, Ensaaf, U.S.A has been meticulously collecting data on the disappeared and unlawfully killed, with a mission to end impunity and achieve justice for crimes against humanity.

Continuing and furthering Jaswant Singh's mission, the "Punjab Documentation Advocacy Project (PDAP)," led by the U.K. based human rights lawyer and activist couple Satnam Singh Bains and Jaswant Kaur, has since 2008 uncovered evidence of more than eight thousand illegal cremations from fourteen districts of Punjab. This evidence has formed the basis for a renewed litigation before the Supreme Court of India for a full disclosure of the records of enforced disappearances and extrajudicial killings in Punjab, seized by the Central Bureau of Investigation in 1997-98.

Ram Narayan Kumar, Human Rights activist, writer and cofounder - Committee for Coordination on Disappearances in Punjab

Paramjit Kaur (second from right) with other members of the Khalra Mission Organization protesting outside the Tarn Taran D.C. office, February 2015

The Fire and the Bird

Whenever someone, frustrated by the hopelessness of obtaining justice, questioned the significance of the work Jaswant Singh was doing, insinuating that his efforts were like a drop in the ocean of injustice, he would tell them this fable:

"Once, when the jungle caught fire, a bird would fill its beak with drops of water and empty the water onto the fire. It would then go back and get more, continuing its quest with all sincerity. Someone questioned, 'Silly bird! Will the fire be put out this way?'

The bird replied, 'There are three kinds of creatures associated with this fire: the ones who were responsible for the fire, the ones who are bystanders watching the drama, and the ones who are making every possible effort to put it out. I am content that when the world will tell this fable, my name will not be included in the category that caused the fire or the one that watched it silently, but in the one that dedicated itself to putting the fire out.'

Often, we surmise that our little and lone effort will not make any difference in the grander scheme of life. But history will record and tell in which of the three categories our names will fall."

Jaswant, in the span of a mere forty-three years, lived such an exemplary life that as long as we continue to remember him, little lamps in huts will keep challenging the darkness around them, and little birds in jungles will keep trying to put out fires.

A Page from History

1801- 1839 Reign of Maharaja Ranjit Singh

1914 May 23: Steamship Komagata Maru with 376 Punjabis arrives in Canada

1914 July 23: Komagata Maru sails back to Calcutta

1919 April 13: *Jallianwala Bagh* massacre

1920 December 14: *Akali Dal* formed

1926 March: *Naujawan Bharat Sabha* was founded by Bhagat Singh, at Lahore

1947 August 15: Partition of India, Punjab and Bengal

1952 November 2: Jaswant Singh born in the Khalra village

1955 July 4: Police raided *Darbar Sahib* Complex killing hundreds

1965 September 6: Start of Indo-Pakistan War

1966 November 1: Punjab Reorganization Act, 1966, further divided East Punjab into four parts

1969 Jaswant Singh finished high school

1971 December 3: Start of Indo-Pakistan War

1973 Jaswant Singh moves back to his village after finishing college

October 17: *Akali Dal* adopts the Anandpur Sahib Resolution

1974 Jaswant Singh started job as a *Panchayat* Secretary

1975 June 25: Prime Minister Indira Gandhi proclaimed a national emergency suspending the Constitution of India

1977 October 29: Comprehensive version of the Anandpur Sahib

Resolution passed in the general session of *Akali Dal's* meeting at Ludhiana

1978 April 13: Sikhs, Nirankaris clash in Amritsar, 13 Sikhs killed

Sikh political organization – Dal Khalsa, formed with the objective of Sikh sovereignty

September 25: Police fired upon a protest march against Sant-Nirankari cult, in Kanpur. A dozen lives were lost and over 70 Sikhs were injured

1980 April 24: Nirankari cult leader assassinated

1981 August 19: Jaswant Singh married Paramjit Kaur

September 20: *Sant* Jarnail Singh Bhindrawale was arrested on charges of terrorism

September 29: Air India plane hijacked to Lahore. Hijackers demand release of *Sant* Bhindrawale

1982 August: *Dharam Yudh Morcha* formally launched by *Sant* Bhindrawale

1983 October 10: Prime Minister Indira Gandhi imposed President's Rule in Punjab

1984 May 24: Akali Dal announced intensifying their movement against central government from June 3, 1984, the day of the *Shaheedi Gurpurab*

May 25-31: Government deployed about 100,000 troops throughout Punjab encircling historical and popular gurdwaras, as *Akali* volunteers mobilized towards Amritsar

June 1-6: Operation Blue Star - assault on the *Darbar Sahib*
October 31: Prime Minister Indira Gandhi assassinated

November 1-3: Sikh bloodshed and lootings – the third *Ghallughara*

1985 July 25: Rajiv Gandhi-Harcharan Singh Longowal Peace Accord signed

1986 January 26: Government backtracks from Peace Accord

January 26: *Sarbat Khalsa* passed a *Gurmatta* asking the Sikhs to break shackles of slavery and injustice from India

April 29: Another gathering at *Akal Takhat* declared the creation of Khalistan – a sovereign Sikh nation state

April 30: Government launched Operation Black Thunder - I

1987 May 11: Central government imposed President's Rule in Punjab dismissing *Akali* government

November: Jaswant Singh resigned from the position of *Panchayat Secretary* in protest against human rights violations by the government

1988 May 9: DGP K.P.S. Gill launched Operation Black Thunder - II

1991 Jaswant Singh migrates to England, seeking political asylum

Punjab brought under the Disturbed Areas Act giving security forces even more power to search, detain and interrogate anyone without a judicial warrant

1992 January: Elections in Punjab, boycotted by *Akali Dal*
Jaswant Singh returns to India

December 6: BJP activists demolish Babri Mosque

1995 January 16: Jaswant Singh and his companions address a press conference alleging that the police and security forces in Punjab had engaged in illegal abduction and murder of innocent people, holding K.P.S. Gill responsible for it.

January 18: K.P.S. Gill refutes the allegations in a press conference

February 27: Jaswant Singh, in a press conference, publicizes the threats to his person warning the state that eliminating him would not put an end to the matter of 25,000 enforced disappearances

April - July: Jaswant Singh traveled to Canada, England and Austria

June 1: Jaswant Singh addressed the Canadian Parliament

July 26: Jaswant Singh returns to Punjab despite escalating threats and his well-wishers' attempts to stop him from going back

August 31: Chief Minister Beant Singh assassinated in Chandigarh

September 3: Jaswant Singh visited his parents in the village Khalra for the last time

September 6: Jaswant Singh picked up by security agencies, and kept in illegal detention

September 6: Paramjit Kaur tries unsuccessfully to lodge a complaint with the police

September 9: Paramjit Kaur files a petition before Supreme Court

October 28: Jaswant Singh was shot dead, his body dismembered and dumped into the Harike Canal

November 15: Supreme Court directed the CBI to investigate Jaswant Singh's abduction and the allegations leveled in his January 16, 1955 press release

1996 July 30: CBI submitted the report holding nine officers responsible for Jaswant Singh's abduction and disappearance

1997 May 24: SSP Sandhu commits suicide

1998 March 2: SPO Kuldip Singh records his testimony providing the breakthrough that led to convictions later

2005 November 18: Six Punjab Police officials convicted and sentenced by the CBI Court – two were awarded life terms and four others sentenced to seven years imprisonment

2007 High Court changed the sentence; five of the six convicted were given life sentences and one was released

Resources

Reading:

- Reduced to Ashes - The Insurgency and Human Rights in Punjab - Final Report: Volume One - Ram Narayan Kumar, Amrik Singh, Ashok Agarwal and Jaskaran Kaur, South Asia Forum for Human Rights (2003)

- Deaths and Enforced Disappearances During the Counterinsurgency in Punjab, India - A Preliminary Quantitative Analysis - Romesh Silva, Jasmine Marwaha, Jeff Klingner, Benetech, Ensaaf (2009)

- Twenty Years of Impunity - The November, 1984 Pogroms of Sikhs in India - Jaskaran Kaur, Ensaaf (2004)

- Oppression in Punjab - Citizens for Democracy (1985)

- Lost in History : 1984 Reconstructed - Gunisha Kaur, Sikh Youth Federation (2009)

- Twenty-five years on...1984 Sikhs' Kristallnacht - Parvinder Singh, Truth and Justice Campaign (2009)

Activism:

- Khalra Mission Organization, 8 - Kabir Park, PO Khalsa College, Amritsar - 143002, India

- Punjab Human Rights Organization, H. No. 22, Sector 2, Chandigarh, India

- Ensaaf [ensaaf.org]

- Punjab Disappeared [punjabdisappeared.org]

Acknowledgement

I must thank my friend **Parmjit Kaur Mahal** for bringing this project to my lap, and to **Navkiran Kaur**, daughter of Jaswant Singh Khalra, for providing details on Jaswant Singh's life that have never been previously documented, as well as making precious family photographs available.

I have relied heavily on previous works by **Ram Narayan Kumar** and his team (Reduced to Ashes), and that of **Paramjit Singh Gazi** (Sikh Shahadat), as well as Citizens for Democracy's report (Oppression in Punjab), and **Gunisha Kaur**'s book (Lost in History, 1984 Reconstructed). I am thankful to **Sukhdeep Singh Barnala** for his guidance as well.

I thank **Shelby Steinhauer** and **Gayle O'Shaughnessy** for editing the English text.

I am grateful to **Parvesh Sharma** for helping me with Punjabi translation and **Nirvair Singh** for editing the Punjabi text.

I am immensely thankful to the art team for bringing the text to life - **Amandeep Singh, Inkquisitive** for his beautiful illustrations, **Gurdeep Singh Dhaliwal** for graphic design and **Navkiran Kaur** for helping me with Art direction.

And lastly, I must thank **Rafaqat Ali** for his wonderful direction on the book and keeping me motivated.

Gurmeet Kaur

About the Author

Gurmeet Kaur is a children's author, storyteller and teacher of the Punjabi language. She has authored and published the book series *Fascinating Folktales of Punjab*, the first bilingual, illustrated book series that has created a new wave of interest in children's literature on Punjab.

A mother of two, Gurmeet switched from her twenty-five years long Software Engineering career to being a full-time publisher and an activist for Punjab and the Punjabi language. She lives in Atlanta, GA, USA.

About PIPPAL

Partnership in Promoting Punjabi Art and Literature (PIPPAL) – a U.S. nonprofit organization was formed in 2013 to serve as a forum for promoting and popularizing Punjabi language amongst young generation by producing appealing art and literature.

During the last seven years, PIPPAL, through its project, *Fascinating Folktales of Punjab*, has successfully reached thousands of young children and their parents all over the world, instilling in them a love for the richness and beauty of the Punjabi language and literature through its nine illustrated books in printed and audio formats.

These books preserve ancient folktales and their life-lessons, along with authentic Punjabi language, artifacts, life-style, flora, and fauna of Punjab through vivid illustrations and poetic text. They act as great tools to connect generations and make excellent dual-language (Punjabi-English) learning resources for schools worldwide.

Connect with us

www.pippal.org, www.folktalesofpunjab.com

info@pippal.org

www.facebook.com/pippalorg

www.instagram.com/pippalorg

Khalsa was formed
to defend the
fundamental rights
of all human beings.
If you are not able to
defend your own human
rights, you cannot define
yourself as Khalsa.

Jaswant Singh Khalra

MESSAGE

Paramjit Kaur, wife of Jaswant Singh Khalra

This book is in itself a history of the twentieth-century Sikh struggle and will be a force guiding the youth of the *panth* forward.

Those high on power and political dominance assumed oppression was their right. On the frontline, it was Sardar Jaswant Singh Khalra's mission to defy the government's tyranny; not to lament, but to hold it accountable through legal means without taking the law into his own hands.

I held my breath while reading the entire book; I felt the words were my own. Gurmeet Kaur has taken this task on with great care, understanding the pains of Punjab and our *panth*. The beautiful artwork and historical pictures help further the subject matter understanding.

Paramjit Kaur
Patron - Khalra Mission Organization
Amritsar, July 5, 2020